God Loves an Unmade Bed

Spirituality for the Imperfect

Father Tom Allender, S.J.
Donald C. Fisher

D0051301

Published by:
Life's Journey Marketing
12307 E. 53 rd St.
Kansas City, MO 64133
(800) 548-1029 / info@lifesjourney.org

Editor: Andrew Elliot
Book design and production: Marilyn Hager
Cover illustration and design: Marilyn Hager

Printed in the United States of America

Publisher's Cataloging-in-Publication Data
Allender, Tom. Fisher, Donald.
God loves an unmade bed : spirituality for the imperfect /
by Tom Allender and Don Fisher.-- 2nd ed.

p.cm.
LCCN: 99-
ISBN: 0-9675948-0-4

1. Spiritual life--Catholic Church. 2. Spirituality--Catholic
Church. I. Fisher, Don, 1958- II. Title. Addiction.

BX2350.65.A45 1999

248.4'82
QB199-1612

To Ashlee, Ryan, Molly, Samuel,
and their generation.

Acknowledgments

We would especially like to acknowledge the following people for their help along the way: Ed and Michelle Robson, Bill and Edith Pulice, Mary Jean Tanner, Dan Drackett and all our many friends through the years.

Special thanks to Ed Robson, without whom this book would not have been possible.

CONTENTS

Preface. ix
Introduction 1

PART I   **FEAR AND FAITH**
Chapter One   Being Comfortable in Our
                         Own Skins 11
Chapter Two   Living Our Dramas 25

PART II   **THE CAPITAL SINS**
Chapter Three   Pride. 37
Chapter Four   Avarice. 47
Chapter Five   Anger and Resentment 55
Chapter Six   Lust 65
Chapter Seven   Envy. 71
Chapter Eight   Gluttony 75
Chapter Nine   Sloth. 81

PART III   **OUR EXPERIENCE OF GOD**
Chapter Ten   God Loves An Unmade Bed. 93
Chapter Eleven   Powerlessness, Surrender,
                         Transformation 109
Chapter Twelve   Emotional Honesty 133
Chapter Thirteen Giving God A Gap 141

PART IV   **PRAYER**
Chapter Fourteen Conscious Contact—
                         The Importance of Prayer 165

PART V   **PRIORITIES FOR BUILDING A**
                      SPIRITUAL PROGRAM
Chapter Fifteen   Our Spiritual Program—
                         A Needs List 187

A Final Reflection 217

PREFACE
by Don Fisher

Father Tom Allender and I met hiking on a mountain eighteen years ago. Looking back, I believe the circumstance of our meeting was symbolic of what was to come. All of us have mountains to climb.

We are quite a combination, living proof that God works in mysterious ways. Tom was in his mid-forties, a popular teacher and priest. I was a single, twenty-four year old firefighter and paramedic. I became inspired due to the pain that I felt when two of my dear friends committed suicide within months of each other. These tragedies were catalysts in my search for a more meaningful spirituality. I hoped to discover and share with others anything that might help to prevent such tragedies.

I believed that together, Tom and I could make a difference. In 1986, we created a nonprofit company "Life's Journey", a forum with which to share our spirituality. I knew that I needed practical spirituality to stay centered. Father Allender's dad, Ray, used to say, "If you don't keep it awfully simple, it gets simply awful." These words help guide my life.

Spirituality is the road map that, time and time again has guided me out of the desert into the "promised land." It can and will do the same for others. Tom told me many years ago that I would have to know my song well before I started singing. After having gone through some of life's painful experiences, I'm beginning to know my song.

For me spirituality is simple; I pay attention to where and how I send my spirit to others. I also notice how I am receiving the spirit from others. If you would like to get in touch with the powerful effect spirituality does have, think back to someone who believed in you, someone who helped you believe in yourself, reflect back on what that experience has meant in your life. You carry their spirit with you and always will.

Jesus said, "The way we measure it out is the way it is measured back to us." To me, "measure" implies that I must be conscious of the spirit I'm sending. Prior to developing a spiritual program, all I could do was react and I usually gave to others what they gave to me. If they gave me anger, that's what they got back; and likewise if they were kind to me, I reacted accordingly. Jesus calls us to pay attention to where and how we send our spirit to others as well as to be conscious and considerate of the type of spirit others are sending us. All of our relationships are mirrors of the relationship we have with ourselves. When I can look at the reflection that others are sending me, I have discovered that I'm receiving what I have been giving.

I realize today that if I am restless, irritable, or discontent, I need to ask God for help, instead of blaming others or making excuses. When Jesus said, "Knock and the door will be opened, Seek and you will find," he was giving us directions. I'm amazed at how quickly I forget to ask for God's help, especially in the midst of chaos or confusion and instead get busy with my own agenda.

The first step in becoming spiritually responsible is simply to remember to stay humble before God. In my past, I was usually so concerned about me that I could not pay attention to you. I became spiritually able to respond to people, places and things with a new attitude; this has made all the difference in the world.

With a new perspective, it has become much easier to recognize God's grace. I know when I have a sense of gratitude, I am more able to recognize God's footprints and more likely to give credit to the ALMIGHTY. Today with God's grace I am able to be more honest and, with occasional glimpses into my denial, I'm becoming able to see my own part in negative situations. I've heard it said that there are no victims only volunteers; when I'm willing to look at my part in things, I am no longer the victim. Only with this insight was I able to repent and to begin the healing process.

Prior to developing a spiritual program, I was like a ship without a rudder. Spirituality allows me to do more than just survive. When I am working with my spiritual program, I have intimacy with God, which allows for intimacy with others. When I stopped running from my feelings and discovered what it meant to be emotionally honest, to be vulnerable, God transformed my life.

Today my spirituality provides two things: First and foremost, it provides intimacy in my life, and secondly, it leads me out of my deserts. These deserts, although they've been painful, have led me to a deeper spirituality and provided the most opportunities for me to grow as a person. Life is full of difficult situations, surprises and struggles. Spirituality can help me grow from them all. I can recall a divorce which brought with it a sense of failure, fear for my children and plenty of unresolved anger. Looking back I can see that I lacked the spiritual tools to stop and process my feelings. I've since discovered the power of forgiveness and the healing that takes place when I practice a spiritual program in all my relationships.

It has not always been this way; I ran from my feelings, filling my life with activities and distractions. God found a way of getting my attention.

It occurred when I went into the hospital for routine, outpatient knee surgery. Eight hours after returning home, I found myself feeling very ill. I returned to the hospital only to find that I had been exposed to group A streptococcus, better known as flesh eating bacteria. Five days later, I found myself in ICU on what could have been my deathbed. I received the Sacrament of the Sick. When people came to visit me, they talked in hushed tones. To make this even more complicated, my wife, Kelly, was six months pregnant with our first child. Seventeen surgeries and over a month later, I left the hospital with a long rehabilitation ahead of me.

While in the hospital, and when confined to my bed at home, I was forced to confront myself. I was alone, afraid and in intense pain both physically and emotionally. I found that medication took away the pain. It became my escape.

Whenever we take the easy way, it often becomes the hard way. This proved true, and my drug use made all my problems worse. For some time I lived in denial, but at age thirty-seven I found myself in treatment.

Today, I know what it means to surrender because this process continues in order for me to maintain my conscious contact with God.

When I face unpleasant or difficult challenges, I know God is within to give me strength. In fact, an important aspect of our ministry today is to reach out to support families who are going through similar difficulties. For those currently experiencing struggles with alcohol or drugs, we like to help; please contact us. Information regarding the schedules for our talks are available on our website;

http://www.lifesjourney.org
Or call 800-548-1029

I thank God for my four beautiful children and for the love and support of my wife, Kelly.

In the future, if it be God's will, I hope to become a deacon in the Catholic Church and continue our ministry. I am grateful for the relationship Tom and I have had and I feel a responsibility to share how God's Love works in all our lives.

Father Tom and I enjoyed writing this book together. He assumes the role of narrator through the rest of the book as we share our message of practical spirituality.

Don Fisher
President, Life's Journey

INTRODUCTION

The Pharisees asked Jesus when the Kingdom of God would come and where. Jesus' answer was: "The Kingdom of God does not come in such a way as to be seen. No one will say, 'Look, here it is!' Or, 'There it is!' Because the Kingdom of God is within you."

—Luke 17

Today, spirituality has two objectives. The first is to help guide us through our deserts. The second is to create intimacy. In order for me to have intimacy with God, I first have to have intimacy with myself. When I can become emotionally honest with my feelings, and bring them to God through prayer, and ultimately share them with the people in my life, true intimacy becomes possible. Ultimately, that is what I've always wanted. Spirituality makes this possible.

Spirituality is the bridge of love between God and us. Spirituality can guide us in our most difficult times, when we feel the most alone. We all seem to be searching for a connection to God, one that is real and can be applied to all areas of our lives, especially our deserts. Spirituality therefore brings the power for inner transformation.

Like Moses, for many years Don and I had wandered aimlessly, without a connection to God. This led us to believe we had to rely on ourselves, but deep down I always knew that I was not going to be able to make that journey alone. I knew I was afraid, but found it very difficult to be vulnerable with others.

As a fireman, Don could run into a burning building, while others were running out. But, when it came to being vulnerable with others about his feelings, he lacked the faith and spiritual courage to share his feelings with others. Of what was he so afraid? Wasn't it the common fear that if anyone ever knew us, they wouldn't love us? Jesus told us about the Kingdom within. For both Don and myself, today our spiritual journey starts by asking God for the courage to look within, to make the connection between our thoughts and feelings, and bring these to God.

I have spent most of my adult life running from one distraction to another which had kept me from the Kingdom within. But there has always been a yearning, a deep call for intimacy. I knew I longed to be fulfilled, but no matter what I had accomplished, who I had become, there remained a hole in my soul. Eventually the distractions ran out and I was faced with myself. That's when I began to discover spirituality.

Saint Paul's life is an example of how spirituality can change the heart. Before his conversion, he persecuted Christians, but in spite of this God continued to call him. Paul responded and became an instrument of God's Love and an inspiration to new Christians. He became the most prolific evangelizer of the Gospel.

After his conversion, Paul was arrogant. He had all the answers. He wanted to be in charge. But the more he experienced trials such as shipwrecks and prison, the more he went through the desert and the more he discovered God's Love. This love and forgiveness transformed Paul's life. He became kind, patient, and compassionate as he became a channel of God's Love.

Spirituality made all this possible. Three aspects of spirituality—God's Love, Paul's response to this love and the continuing struggles—transformed his life.

We are each born into the world without a sense of identity. As newborns, we don't feel separate from the world. We are expressions of God's Love. For example, Don and his wife Kelly recently had a baby boy named Sammy who has an amazing sense of contentment and belonging. He appears to feel no separation from the world or the people around him. His love is given and received freely. It is obvious Sammy wasn't taught how to love; love simply flows through him. There is a real connection between God's love and this child. The power of God's Love radiates from within him. Don simply looks at him and receives his love, and he in turn, receives Don's love.

Like Sammy, we come into the world filled with God's Love. We are not separate. As we grow, our parents must get back to their lives, so they can't respond to our cries as quickly as they once did. As our awareness develops, so does our sense of separation and isolation. When we come to realize that we are not connected to our parents, that we are not one with them, we begin to experience the fear of abandonment. Parents are our "gods"; as children we do anything to be loved by them. Our realization that they can leave us creates the tension between fear and faith: the love from within and the fear from without.

As we begin to realize our individuality and separateness, we believe that the love we seek must originate from the outside. We grow older and feel more and more alone. We look to our parents for love, initially, then to our peer groups, then to our marriages, our families and our occupations. We have a need to belong or be in a relationship with others. It is only after we have exhausted ourselves searching for these external connections with people, places and things, that we become willing to accept God's Love.

The desire to reconnect with our Creator is within all of us. If we are ever to be truly fulfilled, and find peace and contentment, we must make the spiritual journey. This book is about how we become separate and how we can all take the path to reconnect with God's love within us. In these pages, Don and I share what we've discovered on our own paths back to God.

As we continue our spiritual journeys, we, like Saint Paul, are challenged to accept the suffering that results from living in the appearance world. Most of us don't want to accept these daily realities. We think our lives should consist of one happy day after another. When we see loved ones in pain, we want to take their pain away. These attitudes begin in childhood. If we grow up in families in which our outer beauty is stressed more than inner beauty, we become alienated from our feelings and the real people we are.

Most of us never become comfortable in our own skins. We think whatever masks we wear are real. We put our energy into the appearance world, without regard to how we truly feel.

What makes us real as persons is placing a high priority on what is inside. We are real when we are in touch with our feelings. As used in this book, personas are not connected to their feelings; they are concerned with how things appear. For personas, as long as things appear to be going well, that's what is important. In these times, a good example might be people who spend their precious time and energy jogging and exercising while ignoring the stresses that harden their hearts.

When teenagers get into trouble, their parents often have different sets of reactions depending upon whether or not others had seen what had happened. If others didn't see their children causing trouble, the parents reacted differently than if the problems had been publicly observed. In the same way, if parents think that good parenting means protecting their children from problems, they create comfort zones. When children have problems and the parents enable them to escape the consequences, the parents are helping the children to avoid pain. This avoidance is often at the expense of learning valuable lessons.

When we consider why we have pain, it is to alert us to situations that may result in either emotional or physical injury. When we lose the ability to sense pain, the results can be devastating. For example, consider how difficult a divorce can be for a child. If the parents refuse to acknowledge the child's feelings, and instead give toys as a distraction, the child only stuffs his or her feelings. Eventually these stuffed feelings manifest themselves in unhealthy ways. This is also true for adults who look for comfort zones in food, drink, sex, and material things. The feelings that are being avoided do not disappear.

Most of us reach adulthood being more concerned with how we appear than who we really are. We often believe that life should be free of suffering, so we seek to escape difficulties rather than owning our problems and working through them. It is possible to change this perspective. We mature spiritually when we see our problems as opportunities to grow, real experiences in which we accept that we're not perfect, that we have weaknesses, and that life is difficult; these become opportunities to connect to God. We allow into our lives a God who lets us be ourselves. God gives us the strength and courage to work through our difficulties and discover truths. Looked at in this way, a spiritual journey is a surrender to a loving God.

To summarize: We come into the world feeling connected. As we gain identity, we realize we're separate from others, but still have the need to belong. Our realization of being separate results in the fear of abandonment. Most of us then go on to experience conditional love in our families. This is where we learn to deny our feelings and create personas. Whenever we can't or won't share our true selves with others, we experience isolation and pain. We try to alleviate the pain by creating comfort zones. But no matter how comfortable our zones may be, they never fill the black holes in our souls. Only when we reconnect with God can we experience wholeness and discover the peace that surpasses all understanding.

This book examines the capital sins, not in a way that condemns human behavior, but as they create isolation. This isolation becomes an opportunity to know our emotions, especially our feelings of anger and fear that can become opportunities to respond to God's grace. We seem to always be much more open when we are in pain. Once we have experienced God's Love, we need to stay connected. We can do that through prayer.

This book also explores practical steps to enable spirituality to flow in our lives. For this to happen, we need to create boundaries. The first step in creating boundaries is identifying what we need. Part of the spiritual journey is learning how to have our needs fulfilled, for only then can we truly be available to meet the needs of others. This process is referred to as building a spiritual program.

> The seed sown on the path is the one who hears the word of the Kingdom without understanding it, and the evil one comes and steals away what was sown in his heart. The seed sown on rocky ground is the one who hears the word and receives it at once with joy. But he has no root and it lasts only for a time. When some tribulation or persecution comes, because of the word, he immediately falls away. The seed sown among the thorns is the one who hears the word, but then worldly anxiety and the lure of riches choke the word and it bears no fruit. But the seed sown on rich soil is the one who hears the word and understands it, who indeed bears fruit and yields a hundred- or sixty- or thirty-fold.
> —*Matthew 13*

Part I
FEAR AND FAITH

Chapter One

BECOMING COMFORTABLE IN OUR OWN SKINS

One day Jesus had gone into the mountains to pray. When it was evening, he came down to the shore to meet his apostles. They were a few miles offshore in rough seas. Jesus came toward them, walking on the sea. They were terrified. "It is a ghost, it is a ghost," is what they said. Jesus spoke to them, "Take courage, it is I; do not be afraid." Peter said to him in reply, "Lord, if it is you, command me to come to you on the water." He said, "Come." Peter got out of the boat and began to walk on the water toward Jesus, but when he saw how strong the wind was he became frightened; and, beginning to sink he cried out, "Lord, save me!" Immediately, Jesus stretched out his hand and caught him and said to him, "Oh you of little faith, why did you doubt?" After that, they got into the boat and the wind died down.

—Matthew 14

When faced with adversity, Peter, like the rest of us, started to have doubts. The spiritual struggle is between the love within and the fear without. It's the struggle between fear and faith. Love comes from God. But how do we learn to be afraid? There are many causes. One of the causes of this fear comes from our experience of conditional love. Conditional love leads to the fear of abandonment.

We can learn much from the contrast between conditional and unconditional love. Consider married individuals who love unconditionally. They each have had a personal experience of God's Love. They believe God loves them as they are. We want to stress here that, though they have begun this journey, it is far from a finished product. They believe in a God who lifts them up. They have surrendered the guilt of the past, have acknowledged their fears, and have become aware of the power of resentments to destroy both themselves and others. They have invited God's Love to enter into their yesterdays. Because of their faith, they are able to name their angers, guilts, and fears on a daily basis.

We say that they are *current* in their feelings, so they can surrender one feeling at a time. They are not tied into a whole system of guilt, angers, and fears that are rooted in the past.

Couples who love unconditionally give the gift of love to each other as husbands and wives. When they let each other down or hurt each other, they know that their spouses are usually there to help them. When problems occur, they generally do not make situations worse. This is not an absolute truth since developing unconditional love is a process; it takes time, but eventually married individuals know that their spouses are there to accept them. All marriages encounter painful moments, even tragedies. It is in moments such as these that couples grow together or drift apart

These couples trust their weaknesses to each other. This spirituality is shared with their children. If you have been around children, it is obvious that none of them are perfect because they all get into messes. Yet parents can love their children the way God loves them and the way they love each other. When they do, their children learn that God's love is within to care for them, especially in their struggles. Their children grow up with a sense of their being special. They have faith in a loving God.

I've met people who have had this deep faith ever since childhood. They've learned to reveal their feelings naturally. They have no fear that others might react negatively. They feel safe, even when they express anger or dissatisfaction. A supportive environment in childhood nurtures a belief that they have the right to experience and express their reality. A loving environment also creates a loving atmosphere for the family meal and the family activities, and makes for a real sense of belonging. A supportive environment also diminishes the need to look to the outside to supply our meaning.

Unfortunately, most of us do not grow up in such an environment. Most parents haven't achieved this level of spirituality. Many are just holding it together. Parents set up rules and expectations; when their children fail to meet these expectations, the parents take it personally.

I remember when I was five years old my parents had a very sacred room, the front room. Since my dad was in the furniture business, both my mom and dad would select very nice furniture for this room. It was off-limits for the children. I don't know how it happened, but one day I found myself playing around the desk and knocked over the inkwell. All the ink fell onto the carpet. I foolishly tried to clean it up with a paper towel, to no avail. I can still remember the terror I felt as I waited for my parents to return home. I was experiencing as much of a living hell as a five year old can go through. I know I spent the next few days in the "doghouse."

How often have parents expressed to their children, "How could you do this to us?" Hearing such words, children begin to fear their parents' reactions. They no longer feel it's safe to disagree or express anger in the home. As these children grow, they become angry and afraid, but are unable to voice these emotions. They have no alternative but to stuff their feelings. Consider the many things children can be angry about today: the breakdown of the family, both parents working, and coming home to an empty house to name but a few. These kinds of factors leave children feeling very alone and afraid. As a result, they grow up feeling isolated.

To understand how our own childhoods might still affect us, it is helpful to reflect back and recall our biggest messes. When things went wrong, what were our biggest concerns: To grow from our painful experiences, or to be afraid of our parents' reactions? If fear was our strongest reaction, it evolved into the fear of abandonment. For most of us, this process began very early in life, when it felt like our parents had abandoned us, when we were most vulnerable. In order to bury our fear of abandonment and win the love of our parents, we created personas or masks to please them. These personas were based less on our own feelings and more on the feelings of our parents. In other words, we took on our parents' feelings and denied our own. We then began a long journey of wanting all the important people to like us, beginning with our parents. We did this because our fear of their reaction took precedence over our need to be ourselves.

Conditional love has a partner in crime, silent praise, and it can also be devastating. I was raised with silent praise. When I did something right, my dad didn't say a word; there was no affirmation. But he sure let me know if I did something wrong.

So when he didn't say anything, that was supposed to mean he was praising me. That was silent praise.

Some years ago I gave a retreat for eighty couples, including my parents. After one of the conferences, I asked my dad if I was as good as Father Barney. He was a retreat master from the past whom my dad had loved and respected. What I hoped my dad would say to me was, "Nice job, son, I'm really proud of you, son." Unfortunately, he didn't say a word. Two weeks later he told my sister that he thought I was getting a big head because I thought I was getting as good as Father Barney. My dad was always afraid that I was going to get "the big head," so he never complimented me.

Both my dad and I had a sign underneath our mirrors. His said: "I am the problem" Mine said: "I am precious." I don't need to be reminded that I'm the problem; that's my natural reaction. This was a good example of the difference between two generations.

After growing up in the midst of silent praise, I entered the Jesuit novitiate. Jesuits have been called the Marines of the church. In fact, one of my Jesuit classmates left and became a Marine. He told me that, after the Jesuits, the Marines were a piece of cake. As Jesuit novices, we were formed with strict discipline. We were always being told what was wrong with us; very seldom were we given positive reinforcement. As a result, members of my generation rarely complimented each other. Since we were trained with silent praise, we were hungry for approval and rarely complimented our competitors. Similarly, when parents give their children silent praise, the kids grow up in competition with each other, hungering for their parents' approval.

Fortunately for me I have learned from my dad's friends how much he loved and respected me; I had never heard that praise from him directly. Because of silent praise and conditional love, I grew up thinking there was something wrong with me. Otherwise, I thought people would have affirmed me the way I was. After being ordained, I worked under a superior who was much like my father. He always told me what I did wrong. He never told me what I did right. The only time I found out how much he loved and respected me was when I left, and he wrote an article about me in the newsletter.

Such experiences create fear and lower our self-esteem, because we think that nobody likes us the way we are. Later, the fear of abandonment plays an important part in our marriages and friendships, and even our institutions. This fear destroys relationships and is an issue for everyone. Growing up, we are afraid our parents will not like or approve of us, which is a form of abandonment, if we are not the way they want us to be. Later, we fear spouses and friends will leave us if we express feelings that are contrary to their expectations. This fear of abandonment is responsible for the creation of our personas. We learn to act a certain way rather than be authentic; we don't express our feelings. When we hide our feelings, especially our anger, dishonesty with ourselves occurs.

One would believe that honesty with ourselves would be natural and easy. However, because of conditional love, we spend our lives trying to be what other people want us to be, and we become very uncomfortable with whom we are.

Whether it occurs in our families, our friend-ships, or our marriages, conditional love creates fear. This fear forces us to project our fears and angers onto others. We do this because we have not been taught how to go within ourselves and consider our own feelings. A reason we can't go within is that we are dishonest with ourselves. This contributes to our denial system. Therefore, we resist working through our issues. We're fearful that we can't say how we feel, which means we can't be who we are.

Spirituality is there to give us the strength and provide the ability to be honest with ourselves. When we believe that God loves and accepts our feelings, we begin to be emotionally honest with ourselves. When we begin to accept ourselves unconditionally, just as we really are, and just as God loves us, then we can be honest with others. In the end, if we don't begin to know the real self behind the masks, it is impossible to share; thus intimacy remains only a concept.

Observe how many times we put on and take off our masks throughout the day. For example, a teenager who is filled with fear may hide behind the mask of arrogance. An Archie Bunker type may act on the outside like he has all the answers, but on the inside he doesn't even know the questions. Some of the angriest people among us can never even admit they are angry. Thus, if we are unable to own our real feelings, we are left with the alternative of denying them.

Honesty with self is so vital that when young couples start to get serious about marriage, I tell them the most important quality to look for in a potential spouse is honesty with self. I'd rather not witness a marriage until the individuals involved have had a big fight. That is when their true personalities emerge. When we own our own truths, it enables us to begin to change. For example, it might work for a man to be married to a very insecure woman as long as she can admit that she is insecure. However, if she is not honest about her feelings of insecurity, she might spend the marriage making her husband into the issue. That's what we do when we are insecure: we make others the issue.

Similarly, a woman can be happily married to a man who is all tied up emotionally if he is honest with himself. As long as he is willing to admit his emotional unease, there is an opportunity to improve the marriage. However, if he cannot be honest, he will spend the marriage telling his wife that she is too emotional. Honesty with ourselves, being comfortable with our feelings, and a loving God are all intrinsically interconnected.

It is much easier to have honesty with ourselves if we have others to help us. We need the feedback. As long as there is trust in a marriage, the partners can encourage each other to be honest. If they help each other be honest, they can both grow. If, on the other hand, a person is not able to express feelings due to fear of his or her spouse's reactions, honest communication is impossible.

How important are these issues in the conflict between fear and faith? When we hurt somebody we love, when we let them down, are they there to lift us up? Or do they make us feel guilty? We feel terrible when we disappoint the people we love. Usually, when they make us feel guilty, we take out on them all the angers we feel toward ourselves. Difficult times can be the most important moments in relationships. These are the times when people either build bridges of friendship or walls of separation. These are times when the spouses decide if they can trust each other. Times like these are when children decide whether they can trust their parents. If they have disappointed them, are their parents there to lift them up or to make them feel guiltier? I know adults in their forties who can open up to their friends but are still afraid of their parents' reactions.

Besides the fear that comes from conditional

love and silent praise, there is also fear that comes from our culture. When I was a child, this fear came from religion. I did not grow up in a faith community; I grew up in a fear community. As a child, I went to our parish missions to discover how bad I was.

As a little Catholic, I was raised on hellfire and damnation. There were so many ways we could sin. When I was an altar boy, I watched the priests recite the words of Consecration over and over again to avoid a mistake because they were afraid they would sin. Imagine how they must have feared God even in their most sacred moments.

Although today children do not seem to fear God, they still have plenty of fear. It comes from the culture. We've taken the fun out of being a child. Don's eleven-year-old son, Ryan, plays baseball. There are often two hundred people cheering when he's up to bat. If he strikes out, he disappoints them all. In my youth when we played baseball, I would strike out and then walk back onto the field. It was not a major event. We just enjoyed the game. Today we put so much more pressure on our children; athletics is just one example. Today's students complain about academic pressure and the large amounts of homework. Don has mentioned that his daughter Molly, who is only in kindergarten, already has assignments she needs to complete. The list could go on and on. I think we may be using our children's childhoods to prepare them for the economic system because we have made them so thoroughly competitive.

With all the shootings and violence in our schools, fear has become even more dominant. Today's parents have become more afraid, and they pass on the fear to their children. The amount of fear in our culture is apparent in the language parents' use when their children leave the house: "Now be careful when you cross the street." "Don't talk to strangers." This is fear language. Several years ago, Don's thirteen-year-old daughter, Ashlee, told him about stranger danger: that you can't trust anyone who is not family, friend or relative. In fact, members of the younger generation can seem to be very unfriendly to seniors until they get to know them. Ever since they were little children, they were taught not to talk to strangers.

I remember how much I loved the movie *The Dead Poets Society* because the theme of the movie emphasized the phrase *carpe diem*, which means *seize the day*. It is not often that we hear parents say to their children: "Have a good time." "Do something challenging." "Expand your horizons." I think such statements would be much healthier than continually reinforcing the fear we have in our culture.

Because of conditional love and the resulting fear of abandonment, as well as the denial of our feelings, our projections, and finally our personas, all of us have black holes in our souls. We try many ways to fill up these holes. Whatever we use to fill these holes becomes our meaning. For example, the man who grows up never experiencing the approval of his father may become a workaholic, always trying to gain that approval. Work becomes this man's meaning. Or a person who grows up in poverty may have a goal of making money so he never has to experience his childhood pain again. Another person might grow up lonely and seek to find meaning in relationships. This person is probably very possessive. Or a woman who loves being a mother may get her meaning by mothering her children, even into their adulthood.

In my mom's generation, the role of the woman was to take care of the husband. That's how many women tried to fill up the holes in their souls. Their meaning was their husbands. A similar process often happens to men who retire. They had made work their meaning. Without it, they felt useless and empty until they went through the pain to reconnect with God.

We can even use religion to fill up the holes in our souls. Today, among all religions there is a movement toward fundamentalism. Why is there this shift from mainstream religion? It comes from fear. Often, fundamentalists find their meaning in scripture or religious institutions. Religion exists to celebrate faith, not be a substitute for it. The fear that exists today can either bring religious people to a faith in a loving God or drive them into fundamentalism.

Jesus said to his disciples, "Therefore I tell you do not worry about your life and what you will eat, or about your body and what you will wear, for life is more than food and the body more than clothing. Notice the ravens: they do not sow or reap; they have neither storehouses nor a barn, yet God feeds them. How much more important are you than the birds? Can any of you by worrying add a moment to your life span? Even the smallest things are beyond your control. Why are you anxious about the rest? Notice how the flowers grow. They do not toil or spin, but I tell you not even Solomon in all his splendor was dressed like one of them. If God so clothes the grass in the field that grows today and is thrown in the oven tomorrow, will He not much more provide for you. Oh you of little faith? As for you, do not seek what you are to eat and what you are to drink, and do not worry anymore. All the nations of the world seek these things and your Father knows that you need them. Instead, seek his Kingdom and these other things will be given to you. Do not be afraid any longer, little flock, for your Father is pleased to give you the Kingdom."

— Luke 12

Chapter Two
LIVING OUR DRAMAS

Almost all of us grow up with a conditional love that is based on us acting a certain way not consistent with our feelings. We become an actor, playing a role, a *persona*, because we fear that if we don't meet our parents' expectations, we will be emotionally abandoned. Later in our lives, we experience the same fear with our spouses and friends. Being a persona or playing a role becomes automatic. We are usually unaware that we're not being true to our feelings and ourselves.

As we go through our lives, we live in the tension between the fear on the outside and the love on the inside. That love is the source of our being human while fear creates the personas or masks that we show to the world. If we are in touch with our feelings, we make intimacy possible. If we are not in touch with our feelings, we live the dramas of the personas we choose.

I grew up in a loving family, but there were many expectations and a lot of silence. Once, as a boy, I was sick in the hospital, and my parents brought a toy to entertain me. After they left, I broke it. The next day my parents came and asked me, "What happened to the toy?" I told them that the nurses had broken it. I didn't want to lie to my parents, but I didn't think they would like me if I had told them the truth. I was more concerned about my parents' feelings than about living my own truth.

Although later in life my dad had developed a spiritual program and did not drink for his final thirty-five years, when I was growing up, he was still drinking. As a result, I became more involved in my parents' feelings than my own, specifically the emotional impact that my dad's behavior had on my mom. I felt responsible for their feelings. Since I was the oldest, my persona was that of the responsible child. In high school I knew my dad wanted me to get good grades; I thought that if I got all A's, he would quit drinking. I believed my behavior influenced how my dad lived. Since my dad was a football fan, I believed that if I made the football team, he would quit drinking.

Oftentimes, when parents get a divorce, the children believe it's their fault. They think that if they had been better children, their parents would not have divorced. The feelings of the parents and children are thus intertwined.

After the eighth grade, I entered a minor seminary to become a priest. Around that time, my dad's Jesuit high school class had a reunion. The whole family went, and he introduced me to some Jesuit priests. On the way home, my dad mentioned, "Son, I'm so glad you're in the seminary. But, you know, those Jesuits, they are the best." I can still remember the place and the time of day. After that, I left the minor seminary and joined the Jesuits. This is an example of how I continued to get my meaning from trying to please my father.

Years later, before I was ordained, most of my friends had left the Jesuits, and I doubted whether I had a vocation. I went fishing with my dad three different times to inform him that I was leaving the Jesuits. I felt I didn't belong; everything was falling apart. Yet what did I do? I didn't tell him how I really felt. Instead, I told him what he wanted to hear, and I remained a Jesuit. Yet, grace worked in its amazing way, since eventually I found a wonderful vocation, and today I'm a happy priest. However, back then it was more important for me to please my mom and dad than to be true to myself. So I denied my feelings and never shared my truth.

I have always presented the image of having it all together. That's the persona that I have shown to the world: the responsible one who always has to be in control. It's how I received my strokes. It began when I became the responsible child in my family. Then, as a priest, I thought that I was comfortable when I presented the same persona of being responsible and having it all together. However, this presentation didn't work because the mask covered my real feelings. In fact, the more I felt pain, the more I had a tendency to hide and to say, "Everything's fine".

In childhood, I learned three rules: Don't feel. Don't communicate. Don't trust. I learned to bury my feelings and, since I couldn't share my feelings, there was no way for me to communicate. Also, since my parents had so many of their own problems, I learned very early in life not to trust anybody. I learned to solve everything by myself. I denied my need to belong, which precluded any intimacy.

When we are children, our greatest need is to be loved by our parents. But when we enter the fifth grade, we begin the need to be approved by our peer group. How we interact with our peers indicates how comfortable we felt emotionally while growing up in our family systems. All those habits that we developed in our family systems we now transferred to our peer group. If we are football players, we develop football personas. If we're in drama, we develop drama or speech personas. There are many personas we can develop, dictated by the peer groups we choose. This is how we get our strokes. This is when we begin the journey of wanting everyone to like us, especially the important ones.

Later, we take habits we developed in our family systems, which were reinforced in our peer relationships, and bring them into our marriages. The pressure of needing to be liked and the fear of abandonment continue. Often, we pressure our spouses into becoming images of our parents. Also, we can know our children as we want them to be, rather than as whom they really are. We develop a denial system that surrounds our feelings and, since we cannot feel, we are unable to communicate. We can't talk about our loneliness, fears, anxieties, jealousies, or angers. So we bury them and nobody gets to know us. Other people only know our personas so they cannot love what is not real.

Don also developed a persona growing up in his family system. Don has an identical twin that filled the role of being the responsible one. Don became the rebel, which was how he got his father's attention. He further developed his persona in high school, getting attention for being rebellious and priding himself on being a free spirit whom nobody could control.

After going away to college, Don followed in his father's footsteps and became a fireman. Although he did well and was promoted through the ranks to captain/paramedic, Don still wasn't comfortable expressing his true feelings. Through the pain of a divorce and the trauma of a rare disease caused by flesh-eating bacteria, Don continued to deny his feelings. After seventeen leg surgeries, Don began to medicate his feelings with drugs. While this was not the solution, it created a comfort zone. Ultimately Don had to face his feelings and, in the midst of much pain, entered his desert and discovered a personal relationship with God. Don and I were opposites. He was a rebel, and I was responsible. What we had in common was that we both had denied our feelings.

All of us have had the following experience: We know people we don't like in our neighborhoods or at work. Then one day they open up and share something personal about themselves. As a result, we start to get closer because we begin to know them. Generally, we can only love people to the degree that they're willing to let us know them. That's why we can never find intimacy until we are comfortable in our own skins.

Persons are people who are alive, spontaneous, real, and live from within. *Personas* are people who, even if we know them for thirty years, we never know them any better than the first day we met because they're not revealing their true selves.

When we are persons, we can look back at our lives and be grateful. That's one of the differences between persons and personas. Personas look back at their lives and are bitter. Sometimes the bitterness only appears after a few drinks. When we are persons, we can look back and be appreciative for our most painful events. We were not thankful when we were going through that pain, nor would we ever have wanted to go through it again. Yet we had realized that these were the times when we grew spiritually and received God's Love. We had to go through the desert to get to the Promised Land.

Where do we find God? We find God in our deserts.

There is a beautiful story about a person who demonstrated for peace and justice in the sixties. People made fun of his idealism. One day someone derisively asked him if he thought he could really change the world. He stopped for a minute, reflected, smiled, and said, "No, I live the way I live so that the world won't change me."

When we are persons, we look back at our lives and see them as journeys. We see that events of our lives are connected and happen for a reason because God's Love brought everything together. If we are acting as personas, we look back at our lives as a series of separate events; we never discover any spiritual connection.

The most beautiful people in God's creation are older people who are filled with love and wisdom. They're generous and giving people. The ugliest people in God's creation are older people who are angry, cynical, and bitter. They wonder why nobody visits them anymore.

When we are persons, we make real connections with others. We have friends who stay in our lives for years. We develop support systems. We have had the great experience of seeing people we haven't seen for years and talking to them like we had just visited yesterday. We know the wonder of having people in our lives with whom we can share our secrets and our deepest feelings and know that we are loved. On the other hand, if we act as

personas, the older we are, the more we isolate ourselves. We wall God's Love in and wall other people
out. So the more we live, the more isolated we
become.

We all have bad days. Life is not one rosy day
after another. As a paramedic, Don saw many people who, in the midst of traumatic accidents, exud-
ed a certain serenity and peace in spite of pain and
chaos. They were more concerned about helping
others than worried about the damage to their cars.
They stayed in touch with the love inside. Similarly,
as persons of the heart, when we have bad days,
eventually we get in touch with the love. This love
pushes us to go out and do something for somebody else. That's great medicine for bad days
because suddenly we feel good about ourselves. In
giving, we receive.

I have a 1984 Volvo station wagon that has never
given me a problem in over 200,000 miles. It's my
baby. Jesuits don't own anything so this car is the
closet thing I have to a possession. My brother is a
Jesuit in Northern California. At his present assignment there are very few cars available. My brother
has worked in a few cities around Northern
California, so he has friends all over the place. He
has a very rare gift of making people feel loved,
more so than anyone I've ever known. When I'm
out of town, he may want to drive my car so he can
go visit friends. I'm traveling sometimes for seven
or eight weeks at a time, but I don't want to loan

him my car. You know how when somebody else drives your car, they don't take care of it the same way as you do? My car is my baby, and my selfishness tells me that no way am I going to loan it to my brother. However, eventually the love overcomes the selfishness, and my brother can use the car whenever he wants.

After I've been on the road for a long time, I get "churched out." The last thing I want to do when I get back home is go to church. But my Mom loves to show off her son the priest. Many times all I want is a simple mass at home, but I know my mom wants me to go with her. I don't want to go. Eventually, however, the love overcomes the selfishness and I go to church with my mom. When we are persons of the heart, the love is there, and it ultimately pushes us beyond ourselves.

Finally, when we are persons we take responsibility for our lives. When we are personas, we don't. We will never have relationships with God or develop spiritual lives until we take responsibility. Life is between God and us. Until we think we're worth it, it won't happen. Life is what we're doing to ourselves. If we act as personas, we may be filled with anger and fear, and blame others. The more self-pity we have, the more we become wrapped up in ourselves. We become spiritually sick. Just as diabetics get sick if they eat sugar, we get spiritually sick if we become preoccupied with ourselves.

We must have the courage to take off our masks

and share our feelings with the people in our lives. If we learn to share ourselves, as we get older, we become more caring and loving. When we do this, we also make it easier for those around us to risk vulnerability and discover intimacy. The more we reveal ourselves to others, the more we receive from others.

As long as we continue to place all of our energy in the appearance world, we will find ourselves medicating our feelings with objects or activities that create comfort zones. Such behavior eventually manifests itself in one or more of the capital sins. The capital sins ultimately lead us to our deserts. Once there, we can eventually surrender to God. This is the journey from fear to faith.

Suppose Jesus were to meet you on the road. What would He ask you to give up?

Part Two
CAPITAL SINS

The spiritual journey takes many twists and turns. On it, there are many peaks and valleys. We go through pain and brokenness before we are willing to surrender to God. Even these deserts, that given the choice most of us would have avoided, often turn out to be blessings. When we can honestly look at all the areas of our lives without the need for excuses or the desire to blame, all of our experiences can become stepping-stones for spiritual growth.

Chapter Three

PRIDE

Why do you notice the splinter in your brother's eye, but do not perceive the wooden beam in your own? How can you say to your brother, "Brother, let me remove that splinter in your eye," when you do not even notice the wooden beam in your eye? You hypocrite! Remove the wooden beam from your eye first; then you will see clearly to remove the splinter from your brother's eye.

—Luke 7

We often underestimate the power of pride. In fact, the other six capital sins contain pride at their core. For this reason, pride is called "the" capital sin. One of the most damaging dimensions of pride is denial. Don has mentioned people in the midst of a heart attack absolutely convinced it is only indigestion. In my own life, I have witnessed some serious denial. I have helped others with their drinking problems while, at the same time, I was drinking heavily. It never dawned on me that I might have the problem, even though alcoholism was on both sides of my family. Don has a saying "Anger gets me in messes, but pride keeps me there." That certainly has been my experience.

As I now look back over many years as a priest, I have told people to do things with great clarity—and many of these things I should've been doing myself.

When we deny our own feelings, which are our primary connection to our being, we can't process our guilts, fears, and angers. We never invite God's Love personally into our lives. Therefore, we create a persona that is not built on reality. When this happens, we can deny any reality, because we are not grounded in what is real.

I can see this denial in priests who preach the Gospel every Sunday, but who have never questioned whether they believe what they say. I see this denial in married couples that have developed secrets and walls in their marriages, but have become so detached from their feelings that they believe everything is fine. Recently, a man came to me who was devastated because his wife had left him. He believed that his marriage was wonderful, but she felt emotionally starved for a significant relationship. The irony was that he was so out of touch with his feelings that he had no awareness of her feelings.

Therefore, if we have not allowed the love of God to transform our lives, we will build a reality that is both illusionary and deceitful. Pride is a refusal of God's gift of love, a denial of grace.

A few years ago I lost a very dear friend. He was born poor but became very successful. He would do anything in the world for others, but he would never let others help him. He had a deep love for God. He went frequently to church, prayed, and talked passionately about the wonders of God. Yet, he never felt that he was lovable. He was filled with guilt; he never believed God could forgive him. So he loved God, but he didn't let God love him. Eventually, he suffered from severe cancer that changed his life. He became dependent on his wife. She took care of his every need. On his deathbed, he gave God all of his past. He even gave himself credit for being a good person; he believed he was precious because of God's love. He was a man who gave during his whole life, but he had to get cancer to learn how to receive.

When I give a parish mission, I have always wanted to preside over the morning masses because oftentimes the people who go to daily mass have created a system of devotions by which they are earning God's love. The whole issue of spirituality is "Am I doing it my way, or am I doing it God's way?" Pride is a capital sin. Pride is "I have to be in control."

Pride exists when we say, "God, I can do it myself; let me be in control. No thanks; I don't need the gift of your love. I don't require the gift of forgiveness. I don't want acceptance. I'll do it myself." We often demonstrate this attitude at Christmas when we buy everyone else gifts, but don't want anybody to do the same for us. We can give, but we can't receive.

Whenever we give things, we feel like we're in control. Another way we feel in control is by staying with that which is known or familiar. However, we'll never grow if we don't open ourselves to new experiences, new people, new happenings, or new thoughts. It is helpful to ask ourselves if, during the past few years, have we done anything new? It is also useful to make a list of things we've thought about in new ways, or people we've allowed into our lives in more significant ways. We can also ask ourselves what risks we've taken.

For most of us, we always have to be in control. This is the greatest illusion in the world, because we are never in control. It is also dangerous because it stops us from growing. If we look at our relationships with our husbands, wives, and children, are we growing? If we have teenagers, there may be many struggles. Are we growing from these experiences? Or are we going deeper into isolation? It can be a wonderful gift for parents to grow from their experiences with their teenagers. In many ways, these experiences allow parents to see the world through new pairs of glasses. I have greatly appreciated my years teaching high school students because I had to stay young to communicate.

A lot of parents are great when their children are small or when their children need direction. That's when the parents think they are in control.

However, as soon as the children find wings and go off on their own to try new things, the parents become paralyzed. Their homes become battle-grounds because they can no longer control their children. However, these are wonderful opportunities for parents to open up their worlds, to grow, and to hear what their children are saying. If we're filled with pride, if we want to do things perfectly, and if we want to be in control, we won't try new things and we won't grow.

One experience that Don likes to share in our ministry regarding pride was the presumption that he knew what his wife Kelly needed from him as a husband. Don assumed that he knew what it meant to be a good husband, never considering that he should ask his spouse for feedback on what her expectations might be. He lacked the humility to ask his wife what she needed from him as a hus-band. In general, men and women assume that they know what it means to be a good spouse.

Today, Don has the willingness to ask his wife for help in becoming the best husband he can be, and Kelly appreciates him asking. Don has taken this a step further, and asked his children what they need from him as a father. This exercise helped his children to appreciate their own feelings and be able to communicate them with another. Don was helping his children to become emotionally honest. But first Don had to ask.

Are we dealing with the truths in our marriages,

and growing from them? Or have we found safe and secure places to hide? Are we paralyzed by pride in our relationships? Do we allow the ongoing process of growth to happen?

Pride is a refusal to let God into our real selves; it is the failure to receive God's Love.

It is important to differentiate between false pride and true pride. When we feel true pride, we acknowledge our abilities, talents, and achievements. With true pride, we build our self-esteem and feel a sense of accomplishment. If a person at a crossroads of life knows he needs to change, he may look in the mirror and ask himself, "What am I doing to myself?" He may be able to let go of damaging relationships or self-destructive behavior. This point can occur at different times for different people according to their self-esteem.

When we feel false pride, we exaggerate our abilities and act with bravado. We project the opposite of what is real. We act brave, while on the inside we're afraid. Several examples of someone acting with false pride are the man who drives a luxury car and looks down on everybody who drives regular cars or a woman who maintains her sense of control by passing off anyone who disagrees with her as stupid. This is high school mentality carried over into adulthood. False pride is also present in people who walk into rooms and immediately need attention or fish for compliments on their attire or looks because they lack self-esteem.

False pride occurs when we bury our fears, in contrast to giving God our fears. When we feel false pride, we want to be in control. The more that fear runs our lives, the more we have to control. Thus, we always have to be right and have to know everything. We set high expectations; and, when those expectations aren't met, we feel anger.

Do we only enter into conversations when we know everything about the topics being discussed? Do we interrupt other people when they're talking because we think that we're the only ones who have anything of significance to say? Do we always go to restaurants of our choosing and ignore the preferences of others?

Once I heard about a wonderful cruise to Alaska. A travel agent offered me a very good package so I gave him a deposit. I told my family, and they immediately thought it sounded like a good idea. After a few days, one of my sisters called and said, "I don't think I can go." Then my mom and other sister decided they weren't sure if they wanted to go. I blew up. I got terribly angry. I had been full of pride about what a wonderful thing I was doing for them. However, I had neglected to ask them ahead of time if they had wanted to go. I had assumed they wanted to go. I had wanted them to do things my way. I had set up expectations about their responses to my offer, and when these expectations weren't met, I got angry. I had wanted to be in charge.

Our pride isolates us and eventually leads us into our deserts. This is where we can find God. Then we discover God's Love for us and feel how special we are. We realize that we're not here to control people. We're here to share ourselves with people, to give ourselves as gifts.

In the Gospel, Jesus tells us the parable of the Prodigal Son. I have heard the story many times, and every time I hear something new. The story is about two boys and a father. The younger son wants his inheritance immediately so he can go sow his wild oats. He takes off with his money and spends it recklessly until it's all gone. Then a famine comes, and he ends up working on a farm where the pigs are eating better than he is. He realizes that, if he goes back to his father, his father will give him a job, and he will at least be able to eat better than the pigs.

The younger son goes back to his father, not because he's sorry or misses his father, but simply for the selfish reason that he's hungry. The father, on seeing his son returning, does not even wait for him to arrive before he runs to him and hugs him. A great celebration begins. On seeing the celebration, the older, responsible son becomes indignant because all his life he's worked hard and his father has never given him a celebration.

The two sons and the father represent the journey of surrender. We are all three of these people. When we're young, we make a lot of mistakes and spend a lot of time in the desert. Then we move into a period of life when we think we have it all together; we live responsible lives and expect our rewards. As we get older, and we experience God's Love and inner peace, we discover that the essence of life is sharing love with others.

Chapter Four

AVARICE

"Amen, I say to you, it is hard for the one who is rich to enter the Kingdom of Heaven. Again, I say to you, it is easier for a camel to pass through the eye of a needle than one who is rich to enter the Kingdom of God." When the disciples heard this, they were greatly astonished and said, "Who then can be saved?" Jesus looked at them and said, "For human beings, this is impossible, but for God all things are possible." —*Matthew 13*

Arizona has major dust storms. If the windows of houses or cars are left open, even slightly, dust gets into everything. This is a good image for today's materialism. It has penetrated every aspect of our lives. In fact, materialism is the crisis of our age. Ironically, as a priest, I have rarely heard anyone confess to the sin of greed.

Many of us find our entertainment in gambling casinos. Our health care is provided by corporate America. The bottom line in these industries is greed and profit. We are quickly becoming a society of greed, materialism, and selfishness.

I grew up in a society when neighbors looked after one another, when mom didn't work, and we only owned one car. Today we can use a clicker to enter our garage and have no connection with our neighbors. The soccer game has replaced the family meal. Family members can go into their own room to watch their own TVs and work on their own computers. Why has all this changed?

Somehow we've come to believe that material things will make us happy. Ironically, my dad's generation, formed in the struggles of the depression, expected much from their children—our generation, who in turn gave everything to their kids. Today we have a generation of people who believe they are entitled to "things." Many young adults begin with a house that took their parents many years to achieve. They drive expensive vehicles, yet are often one paycheck away from bankruptcy.

I have known doctors who have large families. When they are ready to slow down, their children are entering college. Therefore, they must work harder, usually to send their children to expensive Jesuit universities. The young adults often feel entitled to this education. Recently, a friend confessed to me that he had felt guilty spending so much money on his daughter's wedding. But he acknowledged that he had given her the best of everything, so why shouldn't she expect the best of weddings.

The problem with an entitlement is that we think it is owed us, so we are never grateful. The fact that we're not grateful creates resentment in others. When we are around someone who feels entitled, we often perceive that person as arrogant. Don can recall times when people told him he was arrogant. Because he worked for the fire department helping others, and also worked with people in the church, he couldn't understand how others could see him as arrogant.

For example, despite the fact that he was a medic and saw the results of many car accidents, when it came to wearing a seatbelt, Don felt he was a better driver than others and didn't need to wear his seatbelt. It was not until Don got in touch with his entitlement issues that he could make a conscious effort to discard his sense of entitlement and, as a result, become more humble. What remains unconscious, or we deny, we cannot change. Now Don always wears a seatbelt.

Another example of entitlement has to do with the office of Life's Journey, which Don and Tom have shared. Because Don worked with the fire department, and the office was in a new building, he neglected to take out fire insurance. He thought that would never happen to him. Ironically, while at work at the fire station one night, Don got to listen as fire trucks were dispatched to the burning office. Today, we can laugh, but, at the time, it was a very painful lesson in humility.

I'm not trying to imply that entitlement is only part of the younger generation. In fact, I have some very good examples of entitlement in my own life. This sense of entitlement is based on pride. Since I am in control, I am entitled to whatever I should wish. I deny that everything is a gift from God. We all might want to ask others or ourselves: Do we have entitlement issues?

Just as pride can lead us into the desert, so can avarice, greed, and materialism. Never before has the difference between spiritual values and material values been so apparent. From the viewpoint of materialism, if I have a hundred dollars and I give you fifty, I have less. I lose when I give things away. So I hang onto them. Spiritual values are just the opposite: the more love I give away, the more love I have inside of me. A society, based on material values is, by its very nature, selfish. Spirituality enhances our lives, but if we substitute material things for spiritual things, it never works.

When we neglect to bring our feelings to God and develop spiritually, we stuff them until they are expressed in negative ways, such as the capital sins. For example, many times when wives are angry with their husbands, they go on shopping sprees. Somehow they build self-esteem by buying a lot of things. Or, parents who feel guilty because they don't get to spend enough time with their children may buy them things rather than sharing themselves. This sends the message that things are more important than people. Christmas has become an example of this. Today, children receive more toys than children of earlier generations, but often they have less family.

When children grow up with the sense that things are more important than people, they may believe that the outside world is more important than the world of the heart. If parents give their daughter a lot of things instead of love, she may become a "princess." When she marries, she may want her husband to treat her the same way.

There is always a difference between wanting and needing. When we are materialistic, we think that if we want something, we must need it. Living beyond our means is an easily recognized sign that greed is at work. We use the slogans "Charge it" and "More is better." Greed also exists in corporate America, as exhibited by practices ranging from the depletion of natural resources to the creation of sweatshops in other countries. Other examples include the cutting down of rain forests, strip mining, and the valuing of profits over safety.

Some items that were perceived as luxuries in the past are now considered necessities. Many of us want TVs in every room and two or three cars. Wanting to gain or hold onto things in unreasonable amounts can indicate greed. Spending money foolishly without consideration for what the future may hold, and spending for immediate gratification can also be forms of greed.

When we make material things our god, we create isolation; we also create selfishness. Our attitude

says, "I don't want to share. There's not enough."
Yet we hate selfishness. All of us do. We are thus
participating in an interesting denial system
because we can see selfishness in other people but
have a hard time seeing it in ourselves. Our selfishness, valuing things above people, causes isolation.
This isolation brings us to the desert, where we
have the opportunity to find God's Love.

Once we find God's Love, material things help
us celebrate our lives. If we are in serious relationships, when we go out to wonderful dinners, we're
celebrating our love, not making up for a poor relationship with a good dinner. Material things can
never substitute for the spiritual. When we are
being spiritual, we enjoy people and use things.
When we are being materialists, we use people and
enjoy things.

Jesus said that it was more difficult for a rich
man to enter Heaven than for a camel to pass
through the eye of a needle. Although there are
many different interpretations of this scripture,
Jesus is simply saying that we can't serve both God
and mammon; one has to be more important than
the other. When we are being materialistic, we are
never satisfied. We never seem to have enough. Yet
there are wealthy people who have loving families
because they have made people more important
than things.

As long as we make the spiritual more important than the material, we can find inner peace.

When we substitute the material for the spiritual, we are eventually brought to the experience of the desert, where there is another opportunity to find God.

Chapter Five
ANGER AND RESENTMENT

Therefore, if you bring your gift to the altar, and there recall that your brother has anything against you, leave your gift there at the altar, go first and be reconciled with your brother and then come and offer your gift.

—*Matthew 5*

There is a phrase from Saint Thomas Aquinas that could take a lifetime to understand: "*Quidquid recipitur, reciptiur, per modum recipientis.*" "Whatever is received is received through the mode of the receiver." If we have love in our hearts, everything we hear will be heard through that love. But if we have anger in our hearts, everything we hear will be heard through that anger. The *way* we hear is *what* we hear. If we keep anger hidden in our hearts, it will surely affect everything. Anger is a misunderstood emotion. None of us likes to be angry, but anger is as much a part of being human as love. We often find that when we suppress our feelings, we don't allow them to be part of who we are. We are then not real.

Jesus got angry when he threw the money-changers out of the temple. I don't know whether or not he was having a bad day, but he got very angry. Jesus had many conflicts with people who had hardened their hearts.

Dan and Jeanne's families were in Saint Bernadette's Parish for many years. When they were in high school, they met and became sweethearts. On their wedding day, as Dan and Jeanne knelt at the altar, they were absolutely convinced there was no way they could hurt each other. When they came to mass on Sundays, people said, "If there is any marriage that will make it, it's this marriage. They have something very special." For the first three weeks after they were married, they came home from work and melted into each other's arms. They had dinner with candlelight and flowers and looked into each other's eyes and saw God's immense Love.

About six weeks later, Dan was working hard at his new job, trying to impress his boss. He suddenly looked at the clock and saw that it was 6:30. Normally he was home at 5:30, and he hadn't even called his wife. He grabbed his coat and dashed to the car. He even ran a few red lights on the way home. When he walked in the front door, he was met with the icy silence and the strained voice. Dan tried to explain, but Jeanne interrupted, yelling at him that they never should have gotten married. "I always knew it wouldn't work!" she screamed. Dan looked at Jeanne and wondered why she was so angry. Well, Jeanne had grown up with a father who she had thought was a workaholic. She had always felt second best to her dad's job. So she had saved all this anger from her experiences with her father. Then, when her poor husband came home late one night, she dumped all the anger for her father onto her husband.

Two weeks later, it was Saturday morning and they woke up to discover that their sink was busted. Dan told Jeanne that this was an opportunity for him to learn something so that he could be master of his home. Jeanne pleaded with him to call a plumber. Dan said, "Jeanne please, just trust me." By 10:30, water was squirting in all different directions. They called a plumber. By 4:00 in the afternoon, they had finally cleaned up the kitchen and were sitting down at the table. Jeanne started to tell Dan, "You should have. . ." That was all she got out before Dan started screaming at her, "Shut up, I don't want to hear another word!" Jeanne couldn't understand why he was so angry. Well, Dan had been raised by a mother who always told him how he could do things better. So he had saved all this anger from his experiences with his mother. When Jeanne started to nag him, he dumped all his anger onto her. I often tell couples who are about to be married that they're not marrying each other; they're marrying each other's mother and father.

If we haven't processed childhood anger and if

we haven't owned our feelings, we may project our emotions, making scapegoats out of our partners. We need to look at our marriages and ask ourselves if the anger we have towards our husbands or wives is proportionate to our present reality

Often, when we interact with others, the people who make us the angriest are the people who have shadows like our own. They mirror us. Because we haven't accepted our own weakness, we take our anger out on others. On the contrary, we also find that our anger decreases when we embrace and accept ourselves. Then we allow ourselves and others to be human.

An example of someone not owning her feelings is the woman who gradually becomes very angry while living with a self-centered man for many years. She becomes angry that her partner desires alcohol more than her, that he prefers his friends to her, or that he likes work more than her. She feels unimportant. She accumulates anger because her expectations are not met. If she stays married, her angers continue to grow. She then buries her emotions because she's not supposed to get angry.

If we have been taught never to get angry, we bury our anger and become obsessed with other people's behavior. We ignore our own feelings. We are always looking at the other people's actions. We become victims. If we are being victims, we may use the word *hurt*. "I'm not angry, I'm just hurt." When we make that statement, we do not own our anger. We think we don't have any problems. We are saying that other people are the problem. When we are being victims, we will remain miserable until we release our anger. Yet the greatest obstacle to releasing anger is our fixation on other people's behavior. Sometimes it takes honesty and counseling for us to surrender our anger. If we live with alcoholics or in abusive situations, we naturally develop anger. Oftentimes it seeks revenge.

Males and females can often have different ways of achieving justice. Although it may be logical, male justice is often intellectual. Feminine justice can be totally different. The following example is an illustration of feminine justice: A man saw an advertisement in the paper for a Mercedes that was six months old. The man met with the woman selling the car and drove it. It had very low miles and was in extremely good condition. He asked what she wanted for this beautiful car. She shocked him by stating, "I only want twelve hundred dollars." He quickly wrote out a check and told her that this was a great deal. As he drove away, he felt guilty and knew that something was definitely wrong. When something sounds too good to be true, it usually is too good to be true. He didn't know what was wrong, but his conscience told him he could not take the car at such a low price. He drove back and met with the woman. He told her, "Ma'am, I just cannot give you only twelve hundred dollars. The car is worth much more. I can't, in justice, do this." The woman responded, "Sir, I know exactly what I'm doing. My husband is in Europe with his mistress. He wired me to sell his Mercedes and to send him the money. I know exactly what I'm doing." In feminine justice, we always get what we deserve.

When we acknowledge our feelings of anger, we are less prone to resentments. A successful marriage is a relationship in which both parties can get mad and express their emotions. After both have expressed their feelings, they don't have to think about the situation anymore because they don't take it personally. Processing our feelings rather than burying them is how we stay current. When we stay current, our angers are only related to situations that are taking place in the present. Our emotions are not tied into our *black books* or our past experiences. There are three important steps for staying current. First, we need to acknowledge our feelings of anger. Second, we need to express these feelings. Third, we need to leave no issues unresolved. This means we cannot hold onto anger, keep score, or have black books on one another.

Another reason to stay current with anger is that, if we don't express it, it hides in our bodies. Our unexpressed anger can get stored in tense jaws or can become serious diseases. As Jesus said, "Unless we are like children, we won't enter the Kingdom of Heaven." Children can be playing together and suddenly get into an argument, and ten minutes later be back playing together again. They express anger, but don't dwell on it. If we don't express our anger as adults, eventually we'll take out our resentments on others who do not deserve it.

Once, a woman asked me how to forgive her mother who was seriously ill. She told me about her parents who loved but didn't like each other. The husband found his support system in his daughter rather than in his wife. The wife found her support system in her son. There was rivalry, animosity, and much *triangulation* in the family. The mother could see the defects of her husband in her daughter. One day the daughter had her mother over for dinner. In the middle of conversation, the mother commented to her daughter's husband, "I can't understand why you picked my daughter. There were so many better choices out there."

I helped the daughter forgive her mother. She did the work and let go of the anger. When her mother was dying, she went to spend time with her. Finally, one day she said to her mother, "You know, Mom, I'm very sorry that our relationship has never worked. I've done a lot of forgiving for what happened in our lives. I ask your forgiveness for all the anger that I've had toward you." Her mother turned to her and said, "I don't even want to talk about it." Fifteen minutes later she died and left her daughter a legacy that would trouble her for the rest of her life.

What could have hardened her mother's heart? Whatever it was had probably been passed from generation to generation. Perhaps it was the family system in which she was raised. It could have been many different things. Sometimes people have very bad experiences when they're young and make decisions not to look at themselves, instead focusing on what is outside themselves. In doing so, they reject God's Love. This phenomenon, people filled with anger, resentment, and hatred, is becoming more pronounced in our society with all that is happening to the family.

It is important not only to own our anger, but also to become aware of how to process it. Having anger is human. Burying it can bring us to isolation in our relationships. The only positive aspect is that our isolation can eventually bring us to God.

In the future when we get angry, we might want to consider these questions: Were our responses appropriate for the situation? How did our responses impact others? In the end, would other people praise us for our actions? Or would we be blamed for them?

We need to keep in mind how important it is to accept our anger. We need to process it. We can learn to be angry at the behavior of others rather than at the people themselves. We can work through anger if we have spirituality. Once we're allowed to feel and express our anger, we can surrender it to God.

But, oftentimes before we can do this, we have to understand the power of repentance in our own lives. I'm sure that many of you have had the experience of knowing people whom you thought were good friends. But through their greed and anger, the relationship was destroyed. I have had one very sad experience. But even though I have forgiven them, I do not wish them to be part of my life. I have reflected on whether or not I could ever be a friend with them again. I think I could, if they were to repent. If they were to admit their sinfulness and ask for forgiveness, I could give it. The great irony is that if you were to talk with them, they would probably tell you a story of how they had been so wronged.

My point is not that I am right and they are so wrong. But that, in order for us to be forgiven by God, we must repent, admit our sinfulness, and ask for forgiveness. When we are angry with someone, it's often difficult for us to see our role. We focus on the perpetrator and deny that we played any part in it at all. Upon further review, we usually find that, to some degree, we were selfish, dishonest, or afraid, and that this had an effect on the outcome about which we are angry.

The New Testament began with John the Baptist's message for repentance before we could embrace the love of Jesus Christ. I like to say, *repent or resent*. As long as I cannot or will not see my part, I hold onto my anger, which inevitably turns to resentment. It is important to remember: "It's not whose right, but what's right."

I try to remember that, in my human weakness, I'm going to make mistakes. When I do, I'm going to want forgiveness. You get what you give. So, when we are angry, let us remember to turn the other cheek, change our perspective, and *repent* rather than *resent*. In order to this, we need to overcome our pride and accept our humanness. We are the *unmade bed*.

Often the problems that I have with anger are a reflection of my relationship with God. If I could own my own sinfulness, I would not be so surprised to find it in others. If I could ask for God's forgiveness, I could more easily give it to others. Again, overcoming pride becomes the source of my ability to give and receive forgiveness.

Chapter Six

LUST

He summoned the crowd again and said to them, "Hear me, All of you, and understand. Nothing that enters one from the outside can defile that person, but the things that come out from within are what defile." When he got home away from the crowd, his disciples questioned him about the parable. He said to them, "Are you even likewise without understanding? Do you not realize that everything that goes into a person from the outside cannot defile? Since it enters not the heart, but the stomach and passes out into the latrine. But what comes out of a person, that is what defiles. From within people, from their hearts, come evil thoughts: unchastity, theft, murder, adultery, greed, malice, deceit, licentiousness, envy, blasphemy, arrogance, and folly. All of these evil come from within and they defile." —*Mark 7*

We are probably more dishonest about our sex life than anything else. People spend so much time thinking about it, but so little time talking about it honestly. Much of this is a result of the shame and guilt associated with sex. I think for many of us Catholics, our unhealthy attitudes towards sexuality were shaped as teenagers.

I don't think we have made much progress at integrating our sexuality, our intimacy, and our spirituality. I don't think the approaches of repression or suppression have been helpful. They have only driven the problem underground.

I believe if we learn to listen to our bodies, we can learn to listen to our souls. There is an intrinsic connection between the two. We have to embrace our sexuality if we are going to let God love our "unmade bed," to let God love our sexuality.

In the United States, we inherited a Puritan ethic, all love and no sex. We have become a society of all sex and no love. We have never been able to connect sex and love together. If sex could make us happy or was the answer to life's troubles, we'd be the happiest culture in the world! However, it seems that very few of us have been able to incorporate our sexuality into our humanity. Very few of us have been able to see our sexuality as an important part of our spiritual journey.

When we see our sexuality as a gift from God, it becomes an inner voice that reveals the longing of our souls for wholeness. Can we make our sexuality a part of our spirituality? If we're ever to achieve this, we have to see sexuality as a gift from God rather than as a trial, a punishment, or a secret.

For many of us, sexuality is at the core of our shadow, the part of us that we have never revealed. I grew up with the idea that if I handled my sex life well, I would go to Heaven; if I didn't, I would go to Hell. This concept reinforced my difficulty in believing that our God was a God of Love. How could a loving God have given me this strong desire and, at the same time, been so eager to punish me if I misused it? Sexuality was the only area in which I was not given the freedom to make mistakes and to learn from them. At fifteen, I was supposed to have it all together or I'd go to Hell.

Sexuality has two components: the spiritual and the physical. When two people make a permanent commitment to each other, they celebrate physically and, when appropriate, are open to new life. Their physical union is a celebration of their love and also nurtures their love to grow. It is one of the most beautiful celebrations of the human journey; it produces the greatest of gifts, new life.

However, it is not an ideal world, and sex is not always a celebration. For many of us, it is merely a release of tension. It has a physical purpose. If we hold a lot of anger in our bodies, our bodies must find ways to release that stress, and that can cause us to create sexual energy. That's why, for example, teenagers with a lot of peer and family pressure discover a great deal of new sexual energy. It comes from the stress within their bodies.

If we buy *Playboy* magazines or frequent topless bars, what's really important is for us to stop, take inventories of our daily lives, and spend some time listening to our souls. Maybe we need some time for peace and quiet, or rest, or fun, or leisure. Maybe we've been pushing ourselves too hard, working long hours, filling our lives with too many obligations. If we learn to listen to our bodies, they can tell us about our souls; maybe we have been stuffing too many feelings of fears or resentments. When we try to solve sexual problems externally, we usually make them worse.

A couple that are both 60 wanted to celebrate their 40th anniversary. They decided to go to the beautiful beaches of San Diego. One day while they were lying in the sun, a bottle washed up on shore. They opened it and a genie came out. Because of their anniversary celebration, he offered to grant a request to each one of them. First, he asked the woman what she would desire. She said she'd love to have tickets so that she and her husband could take a trip around the world together. Zap!! They had the two tickets. Then the genie turned to the man and asked what would be his wish. He replied that he would love to be married to a woman thirty years younger than himself. Zap!! He was 90 years of age.

A middle-aged man may enter a relationship with a younger woman. Why? By marrying a beautiful young woman, he thinks that the physical attraction will bring him happiness. This attraction may be a call from his soul inviting him to revitalize his personal life. However, he cannot achieve this revitalization on the physical level, because it is a spiritual issue.

Another so-called happily married man may have fallen into a survival mode, a routine in which there's not much excitement. His spirit is tamed, if not dulled. He can't understand why he's so attracted to spunky young ladies. The reality is that these young ladies represent a part of himself that he's been denying. He thinks that some connection in the external world will bring him vitality. In reality, this revitalization is something he must do for himself.

When we substitute lust for love, the results are often disastrous because our actions lack a spiritual foundation. We may wonder why Christianity is against premarital sex, thinking religion only wants to make us miserable. The truth of the matter is that substituting lust for love does not work.

Consider two young individuals who have fallen in love. They have two feelings: a strong feeling of love for each other and a fear of abandonment. On the one hand, the tension between these two feelings can push the two individuals to communicate with each other, to trust each other, and to develop the foundation of a strong friendship. On the other hand, they can release the tension by jumping into bed. In the first case, any sexuality that is eventually expressed is a celebration of what they have achieved. In the second case, it's a substitute that short-circuits their intimacy. Whenever we engage in recreational sex, we deny the connection between spirit and matter. We are, in essence, disconnecting from God's Love.

Another example is a nice-looking young man with a great personality. He has a beautiful heart and would make a wonderful husband and father. Yet, he's not married and he doesn't have a family. The reality is that he is preoccupied with sex. When he gets involved with a woman, sex takes over. He never develops a spiritual foundation that allows for a permanent relationship. Perhaps this happens because he has stuffed anger toward his father. This anger is released in sexual energy, so he never creates a long-term relationship built on the spiritual foundation of trust, communication, and sharing. Maybe the father never shared his heart with his son, and never taught his son the importance of feelings. This is another example of unresolved feelings manifested as unhealthy behavior.

In summary, our sexual desires can be our souls calling to us from within; they are telling us what we need to develop in ourselves to become whole. This is the beginning of blending our sexuality with our spirituality. The external calls of attractions to others can be special graces from God, asking us to integrate our sexuality with our humanness. If we don't do this, our sexuality will always be secret. It'll never be who we are. Sexuality without intimacy leads to loneliness. A physical connection by itself does not alleviate isolation. That is why the physical can never substitute for the spiritual.

Chapter Seven

ENVY

An argument arose among the disciples about which of them was the greatest. Jesus realized the intention of their hearts, and took a child and placed it by his side, and said to them, "Whoever receives this child in my name receives me and whoever receives me receives the one who sent me, for the one who is least among all of you is the one who is the greatest."

—Luke 9

Envy is as old as the story of Adam and Eve and their envy of the Tree of Knowledge. This story was quickly followed by the example of the two brothers, Cain and Abel.

Are we happy for others when they are happy? Sad when they are sad? Are our emotions appropriate? How do we feel and speak about people who are successful? Is it with sharp tongues or with true admiration? Do we think about the things that we covet, and could we replace the word *covet* with *envy*? We can envy other people's looks, material possessions, intelligence, or anything else about which we feel inadequate in ourselves. Whatever we feel that we lack in ourselves is what we may envy in others.

If we look at others close enough and long enough, we can find things that are very beautiful or we can discover their flaws. What do we want to see? If I'm jealous of someone, I become fixated on his or her flaws. On the other hand, I can observe the same characteristics in the person, yet see something very beautiful about them. What is it that makes us notice the negative or appreciate the positive? It starts with how we look at ourselves.

Jesus said, "Don't judge the speck in your brother's eye until you've taken the beam out of your own." Something that has helped me maintain perspective is the following reflection: *I've never met a person who was more selfish than myself. It's not that I am the most selfish person who has ever lived, but I know myself better than I know anyone else.*

In every act of giving, there is a little bit of selfishness. We wonder what we're going to receive in return. I've never done a purely giving thing. If people knew how critical I could be of them—and I very seldom share this—nobody would ever come near me. What right do I have to condemn someone else when I know myself so well?

If we do not embrace our shadows and do not develop honesty with ourselves, we will never face our own human weaknesses and, instead, will find scapegoats in the people around us. This denial is the root of gossip, slander, jealousy, envy, and all the other negative ways we use our tongues. In our negative society, slander and gossip are almost epidemic. Many of us thrive on it. However, the worst way to compliment ourselves is by tearing down others.

When we hang onto certain people as our meaning, it's amazing how possessive we can become. We are threatened by the idea that other people might take them away. However, these people are not our possessions. The reality is people that we love need a variety of relationships to enhance their growth. So why are we so afraid? The fear of abandonment is at the root of our jealousy and insecurity. Jealousy and envy are actually what push people away. But when we set a person free, love will grow. For example, in marriage, outside friendships help each partner to expand and develop. Then the husband and wife can share that growth with each other.

If we deny our feelings of envy, they turn into jealousy. A good example is what can happen to a father when his wife gives birth to a child. The father may become jealous because his wife is giving all her attention to the baby. So the father thinks that if he gets really involved in his work, his wife will become jealous and give him the love that he needs. Yet, because he has never talked about this with her, she acts just the opposite. She says to herself, "Look at all the energy my husband is placing in his work. He's not giving me the love I need. So I'll put my energy into the kids and make him jealous. Then maybe he'll give me the love I need."

This is called triangulation. We use a third person, place, or thing to create jealousy in others. Ever since we were small children, we have used this form of manipulation. It is a very natural way to try to get what we want. In fact, many of us become experts at triangulation without ever being conscious that we are even doing it.

Whenever our envy turns into jealousy, it creates pain in our relationships. As with the other capital sins, envy and jealousy can leave us isolated and alone in our deserts. However, it's important to keep in mind that this, in turn, invites us to surrender to the God within.

Chapter Eight

GLUTTONY

There was a rich man whose land produced a bountiful harvest. He asked himself, "What shall I do, for I do not have the space to store my harvest." And he said, "This is what I shall do, I shall tear down my barns and build larger ones. There I shall store all my grains and other goods and I shall say to myself, 'Now as for you, you have so many good things stored up for so many years, rest, eat, drink, eat, be merry!'" But God said to him, "You fool, this night your life will be demanded of you, and the things you have prepared, to whom will they belong?" Thus it will be for the one who stores up treasure for himself but is not rich in what matters to God.

—Luke 12

When we find God in our feelings, we discover inner peace and have more balance in our lives, especially in what we eat and what we drink. If we bury our feelings and don't acknowledge them, we may instead medicate ourselves with alcohol or food.

Our society is full of paradoxes. We have so many foods that are nonfat and low fat, and yet we've become so fat. Food and drink serve the purpose of providing us with fuel to keep our bodies alive and contribute to our good health. However, gluttony may be present if we find too much pleasure in what we eat and drink. Gluttony exists when we go to Christmas parties and are preoccupied with the food and unconcerned about the people we meet.

When it comes to gluttony, I'm an expert. I can easily move from one hundred and ninety pounds to two hundred and thirty. I used to be a closet drinker. Very few people ever saw me drink too much, so they never knew I had a drinking problem. When I quit drinking, in a matter of a few months I became a closet sweet eater. Dessert time would come along and someone would bring out a beautiful cake. I would say, "No thank you, I don't want anything. I watch my calories." Then, about ten at night, when everybody else was in bed, I'd raid the refrigerator like Sherman marching through the South. Or I would come into the rectory after a long day and see that someone had given us a prune cake. I love a prune cake. So I would put it underneath my jacket to sneak it up to my room to eat the whole thing.

In my drinking days, I would visit people at the

drinking hour, particularly the people with the best scotch. In my sweet days, I'd visit people during the dessert hour, particularly the people with the best sweets. I wasn't really visiting them, I was visiting their food.

Obvious forms of gluttony are not difficult to identify. Some of us always have to have a drink in our hands. Others are fifty to a hundred pounds overweight. Eating and drinking habits can ruin our relationships and health. There are many reasons why we medicate our feelings with food and drink.

Our parents may have initiated this problem when they told us we had to eat everything on our plates. As we grew older, we may have continued this pattern even though our metabolisms slowed down. Today, the abundance and variety of food in supermarkets and restaurants cater to gluttony in subtle ways. And many of us find ourselves grazing all day Sunday while watching football.

An example of a glutton is a man who goes to a nice dinner. He has hors d'oeuvres, soup and salad, a full dinner, and even dessert. When he finishes and goes home, he spends the rest of the night eating. He's not eating because he's hungry; he's eating for another reason. He may also be compulsive, and stress intensifies the situation. Another man might medicate his feelings with alcohol. This man goes to a nice dinner, has a cocktail before dinner, has wine with his dinner, has an after-dinner drink, and the rest of the night continues to drink. It's obvious there is something wrong. He's using alcohol to escape his unexpressed feelings.

We are becoming more aware that often times overeating and overdrinking are not caused by a lack of willpower but are diseases. Some of us are born compulsive. Those of us who have compulsive personalities live lives of extremes. In doing so, we become self-centered. The things we are addicted to at the moment are the only things that matter. Yet, we all hate selfishness. Thus we begin the journey from self-centeredness to self-hatred.

If we choose to recover in Twelve-Step programs, we are initially filled with self-hate. The more we hate ourselves, the more we have inner pain, and the more we need pain killers. Escapes from pain are often sought via sex, drugs, food, alcohol, which only cause more problems and ultimately more pain. We may spend the evening drinking the pain away, but the next morning we awake with worse problems. We may enjoy the chocolate cake or extra dishes of ice cream, but when we look into the mirror in the morning we feel shame. Addictions and compulsions are really only short-term solutions that eventually bring more complications.

If we find that we are addicted to food or drink, and that we are basically powerless around them, we need to look inside ourselves and see what our addictions are saying to us. Most of us who are drinkers and overeaters are very successful in other areas of our lives. We can accomplish great things, yet we don't understand why our willpower won't work with food and drink. It's very confusing. The answer is that we don't need more willpower; we need to surrender. Until our lives reach this unmanageable point, we are stuck in denial about the real obstacles we must honestly face: self-hatred and self-centeredness. The exact purpose of the 12-step programs is to change self-centeredness to God-centeredness and self-hatred to self-esteem.

Many of us who are recovering alcoholics can look back at our lives and say, "I'm not grateful for all the hurt and pain I've caused, but I am grateful that these experiences have led me to discover a personal God and to face the truths of my life." The pages ahead will stress the journey to powerless, surrender, and inner transformation. The irony is that many of us want to hide from our problems and not talk about them. Hiding only leads to further isolation and pain. Yet our pain and our problems are the source of our growth. When we go through our deserts, we can find our God.

There are spiritual programs of recovery for those of us who have experienced powerlessness in our addictive behavior. As with the other capital sins, experiencing gluttony can, when we are ready, lead us to examine our lives and ourselves. Accepting our human weaknesses is part of the journey toward experiencing God's Love within.

Chapter Nine

SLOTH

Suppose one of you has a friend to whom you go at midnight and say, "Friend, lend me three loaves of bread, for a friend of mine has arrived at my house from a journey and I have nothing to offer him," and he says in reply from within, "Do not bother me; the door has already been locked and my children and I are already in bed. I cannot get up to give you anything." I tell you if he does not get up to give to his friend because of their friendship, he will get up to give him whatever he needs because of his persistence. And I tell you, ask and you shall receive, seek and you will find, knock and the door will be opened to you, for everyone who asks receives, and the one who seeks finds, and for the one who knocks the door will be opened.

—Luke 11

Aristotle taught that the unexamined life was not worth living. Today, the combination of fast feet and denial has created a lifestyle that is unexamined, and unfulfilling. We chase the promise of materialism as if the more we get the more contented we will be. We know in our hearts this is not working, yet we press on. At the end of the day, we are exhausted and spiritually bankrupt. In order to live a spiritual life, we must examine and begin taking responsibility for our priorities, our values, and our lifestyle.

There are many spiritual tools to help us pay attention to our lives: retreats, days of recollection, prayer, spiritual direction, examination of conscience, and the sacrament of reconciliation, among others. We all need help to disengage the autopilot, and *pay attention*!

The list of capital sins began with pride. Sometimes pride drives us to want to do things perfectly. The fact that we can't, leads us to procrastinate. Procrastination oftentimes leads to paralysis. When we're paralyzed, we don't do anything, which leads to sloth. Sloth is a lack of willingness to do the spiritual work. When we experience sloth, we often end up in isolation.

Our relationship with God is a partnership, but we have to do the footwork. What actions are we willing to take in our lives? One of the great problems in our culture is that we substitute talking for doing. This is true for all of us. We can talk about doing things or tell others to do things. We think that by talking, we're actually doing them. Those of

us who are priests, psychologists, and in other helping professions often think that by helping others
solve their problems we are solving our own. The
great danger is that we are substituting talking for
doing. We must ask ourselves: Are we willing to
pay the price? Are we willing to face our truths and
grow from them?

Sadly, I see a lot of marriages about which I say,
I wouldn't want to be in that marriage. Why,
because if I were married, I'd want it to be the best
marriage that it could be. Love is work. It's effort.
Success and happiness are never delivered on a sil-
ver platter! Nothing happens because we turn
thirty or forty. People who attain peace in their
golden years are people who have made spirituality a priority. Marriages are successful because the
partners work at them.

I grew up as a person who didn't express any
emotions. I preferred to bury them; it was less of a
hassle. I took the easy way out, but as with most
short cuts the easy way ended up being the hard
way. Later, I learned to acknowledge and release
my feelings. I developed this process by writing in
a journal. Every night I wrote what was going on
inside me. I knew I had a choice to own my emotions and name them or to bury them. For many
years, I had talked about expressing emotions,
knowing them, naming them, and making them
part of my life. I told every group and every person
in counseling about this process. But I hadn't done

it myself. My change didn't happen until the day I decided that I had to stop running from my feelings. I needed to pay attention to them rather than to bury them. Whether I was feeling fear, guilt, or anger, I needed to write until I released my emotions.

Sometimes I would write a dear so-and-so letter. I'd mention all the things I wanted to tell the person to whom I was writing. I'd let it all emerge. Nothing was censored. I allowed the dialogue to go on inside me and let all the feelings spill out until I felt peace. When I gave the contents of the letter to God, I felt at peace. I never sent the letter. But I had to do the footwork. I didn't wake up suddenly one day and realize that I was dealing with my emotions. My emotional process didn't just happen because I heard somebody else talk about it. It happened because I made an effort to own my feelings.

When I had strong feelings, I stuffed them and became moody. I would remain moody for a period of time ranging from a day to a week. If I became preoccupied with myself, I was more self-centered. The letter-writing process became my vehicle for owning and releasing guilt, fears, and angers. Occasionally I still write, but the process has become more natural.

For a time in my life, I felt very guilty about the past. But when God forgives, he forgets. So I thought to myself, if I haven't forgotten something I did, if I'm still beating myself up about it, that means I haven't forgiven myself. People and circumstances I encountered would remind me of the guilt, shame and anger inside. But I didn't want to live that way. I didn't want these memories to ruin my life. So I said, if God forgives me and forgets, I need to forgive myself and forget.

There is an old story about a cardinal who visited one of the visionaries in his diocese. He wanted her to ask God in her next conversation whether there were any sins that he hadn't confessed. She agreed to do this. Several weeks later, he called on her to find out the answer. She told him that she had asked God, but God couldn't remember. Perhaps we can learn to be as forgiving.

Life is a growing process. Everything that happens in our lives helps us grow. But we have to work at this process. We have to spend time learning to grow. Nothing happens by accident. We have to make the effort, and we have to develop a spiritual program. If we were to pay as much attention to prioritizing our inner lives as we do to building our careers or taking care of our children, we would have magnificent spiritual lives.

One of my biggest challenges was my need to rescue and take care of people. I would discover losers to take care of them. Yet I didn't really want them to get well because then they wouldn't need me anymore. I would go though the process of trying to help people get their lives together who didn't want to get better, so the relationship eventually ended up a mess. They were no better off, and I was nuttier than they were. It was a disaster. I didn't know how to relate to normal people. If people didn't need me, I didn't know what to do. I hadn't discovered the difference between nurturing other people and nurturing their dependencies. Because rescuing gave me my meaning, it temporarily filled the hole in my soul.

I thought love involved making others dependent on me. Later, I discovered that real love involved challenging people to become dependent on themselves. I had to work at that. My awareness didn't suddenly happen one day. I had to replace something with something else. Instead of always focusing on others, I had to develop my own personal life. I had to start being my own best friend. I had to start working on forgiving myself. I had to work on bringing fun and joy into my own life, rather than trying to give them to others. *The great challenge of life is not learning to live with others; it's learning to live with ourselves.*

I had to practice being thoughtful to others. I learned to do the little things—to send my mom roses or a card just because I loved her. I started to do things for others on their terms, rather than on my mine. For example, I learned that my mom appreciated me when I remembered to take the boxes to the storeroom or carry the vacuum up the stairs. This took willingness and it took work.

The beautiful thing about the spiritual journey is

that when we make the effort, it pays off in dividends beyond our imaginations. So much of the effort that we make in the external world never brings back any rewards; it only brings more problems. For example, a man may spend his whole life building his career. He may work countless hours and end up a tired, worn out, old man. What kind of results would he have instead if he spent some of that time building a spiritual life?

Don and I are convinced that work on the spiritual journey brings wonderful benefits because of the discoveries we've made in our own lives. As I go through middle age, the great thing is that I'm just beginning to live. I spent the first half of my life building up my persona. Now my mask is being replaced with a very special and precious person. I am becoming a parent to myself.

When, due to sloth or laziness, we become inactive in our relationships and our productivity declines, we eventually create isolation in our lives. However, this can lead us into the desert where we can reconnect with God.

Unfortunately, in our society many of us see ourselves as victims and refuse to work at our marriages and family lives. We are too absorbed in the external and material aspects of our lives. We take our marriages and our families for granted. Things happened to our families today that could not have been imagined twenty years ago. In the old days, at least we had common television rooms where we all watched television together. Today, many of us have homes where every room has its own television, so we don't even watch television together. Family outings have been replaced with soccer games. So much of this has happened because we have let it happen. We have become products of the culture. Today, if families are going to stay together and marriages are going to grow spiritually, the participants must make much stronger efforts than in the past because the powerful effects of culture and materialism are so prevalent.

There is an important caveat to this chapter on sloth. It concerns the very serious disease called depression. This is an illness that is just as physical as diabetes or arthritis. When depressed, people may wake up in the morning with heaviness that they carry throughout the day, bringing it to their beds in the evening. Oftentimes they are told that if they work at spiritual programs or develop better attitudes, they will feel better about their lives. This is similar to telling diabetics that if they develop better attitudes they can get rid of their disease. It's important for people with depression to take responsibility and obtain proper medical treatment.

At our sixtieth birthday parties, we often act as if life is over and we're just beginning the long walk to the cemetery. In reality, life is just beginning at sixty. That's the challenge. As the adage states, we should not so much fear our lives will end, but that they will never begin.

Each one of the capital sins offers us opportunities to grow from our human weaknesses. They lead us into our individual deserts where, with honesty, openness and willingness, we can reach the Promised Land and discover God's Love.

Part Three
OUR EXPERIENCE OF GOD

Chapter Ten

GOD LOVES AN UNMADE BED

I will not leave you orphaned; I will come to you. In a little while the world will no longer see me, but you will see me because I live and you will live. On that day, you will realize that I am in the Father, you are in me, and I am in you.

—John 14

The unmade bed is symbolic of the messes we experience throughout our lives. How do we move beyond the pain that is part of our human condition? That is exactly what grace is about. When we bring God into our messes, we are making the leap from our own individuality to a belief system in which there is a power greater than ourselves. This is the beginning of our spiritual awakening. Grace can turn our times of despair into moments of peace and contentment. But for this transformation to take place, we must be open to God's Love. Many of us are open to grace only when we are at the end of our ropes, oftentimes as a direct result of one or more of the capital sins.

What do we do when we find that we're at a crossroads? How does God enter into these crucial times? I think the options that God presents at times can be both mysterious and baffling. We call this experience *grace*, which means a free gift. No matter how tragic our lives have become, God's grace is always there to give us strength. Our problem is that we are so self-consumed and overwhelmed that we are unable to recognize it. A quote we often hear is: "God will never give us more than we can handle." I know that in some of my desperate moments, I have felt that this quote was not true because I saw no way out. I was paralyzed with fear.

I like to recall a story in which there was a mouse that was approached by a rattlesnake. It was told by a sequence of pictures that showed the snake approaching and the mouse becoming more and more paralyzed by fear. He literally could not move. If the mouse simply had been able to turn and run, there were many avenues of escape. He could have easily survived this encounter with the snake. But, in the end, the snake simply came closer and closer, to kill the mouse. I think for all of us, God's grace provides us avenues in which we too can escape or begin to cope with situations that have paralyzed us with fear.

We discussed the sources of paralyzing fear and the consequences of the capital sins. I know I was all too familiar with the problem; I needed help with the solution! That is what this book is all about. In order to do this, we need to connect up three realities: God, love and grace. Although God's love is always within us, we have to cooperate with this love for it to become part of our lives. These are what we call graced experience times when we are receptive to reconnect with God's Love.

We already described this experience of grace in the conversion of Paul. We can recall the power of grace in the life of Mahatma Gandhi, who defeated an empire when he stood up to British colonialism with love rather than violence. Grace was a great inspirer of Martin Luther King who fought racism nonviolently. Nelson Mandela, former President of South Africa, is a more recent example of a man who cooperated with the love within and brought together a country that was divided by hate.

Examples of grace can be found everywhere, even on death row. Richard Harris was recently executed in California. He grew up moving from one foster home to another. He was abused physically, sexually, and emotionally. He became an animal and killed like an animal. While he was on death row, he converted to the Gospel. He believed in God's Love, an example of grace. God works in His own time.

We see this grace when a person who has been addicted to drugs or alcohol finally looks in the mirror and asks, "What am I doing to myself? I'm too precious to live this way." We call this "hitting bottom," a moment of grace. In order for grace to work and penetrate our lives, our "persona" must be smashed, leading us to call out to God for help.

And Jesus said to them, "If you want to come with me, you must forget yourself. Pick up your cross every day and follow me. If you want to save your life, you must lose it. But if you lose your life for my sake, you will save it. Will you gain anything if you win the whole world, but you lose yourself in the process?"

—*Luke 23*

When people have emotional breakdowns, these hopefully become opportunities to rebuild their psyches. In much the same way, we often need a spiritual breakdown, a loss of ego, or a deep sense of our own vulnerabilities and sinfulness in order to build ourselves a strong spiritual foundation. These breakdowns can be special moments of grace.

There are many examples of grace in the Gospels. Jesus tells us that it is difficult for a rich man to get into Heaven as it is for a camel to get through the eye of a needle. Then He goes on to mention that nothing is impossible with God, if we cooperate with grace.

Grace not only works within us, but God constantly works in the world around us.

It gets very hot in Arizona. It can typically be in the hundreds-even at night. I spent many long, miserable summers in Arizona. In September, I would leave for my vacation in the Sierras. To get there, I traveled the highway up to Bishop, California, which was the first town that had a breeze and where things were green. Every year, once I reached

Bishop, I would get out of the car and kiss the ground. I was finally back in the human race! I always promised myself that I would give a mission in Bishop to thank the town for being where it was.

Eventually I gave them a mission. I finished the mission on a Thursday night, and then Friday had to drive to San Francisco to catch a plane to Connecticut. In order to get to San Francisco, I had to drive through the backcountry of the Sierras. So I was driving in the middle of nowhere, going around a curve, and I had a flat tire. I had to stop right where people who were driving around the corner could not see me. To make matters worse, I went to get the tire-jack to change the tire, but the jack was useless. I told myself I probably had to wait a few hours for a highway patrolman to come by and, hopefully, I'd be able to make my plane. Three minutes later, a couple stopped their car in front of me. Not only did the man loan me his tire equipment, but also he changed the tire. In fact, if I were doing it, I would probably still be working on it! Then the couple wouldn't take any money as thanks. I was so grateful. It was a Jewish couple from Israel and they were celebrating a holy day, during which they were supposed to do something for somebody else. So, on this particular holy day I was that somebody.

The night before I had the flat tire, a man called me at the church about seven o'clock. He was driving from San Diego to Barstow—a distance of about 250 miles, and he had run out of gas. He had a job waiting for him in Barstow and wanted to know if I could fill his tank. I said, I couldn't do it now, since I have to preach in a few minutes. But at nine o'clock, I'll be available. Later, I filled up his tank and he was very grateful. I think those two events, the man who ran out of gas and the people helping me on the road, were connected. A long time ago Jesus told us that the way you measure it out is the way it's gong to be measured back to you.

Another example occurred while I directed a treatment center for young alcoholics and drug addicts. It was on a ranch located fifty minutes outside of Phoenix. I also still had all my parish duties. Oftentimes, I took the kids to Twelve Step meetings and other places. I didn't have any car except my own. I had to travel on dirt roads. When it rained, there was a lot of mud. Often I was with the kids until late at night. Then I drove home and would get up at six o'clock in the morning. I was getting worn out. I was reaching the end of my rope.

Then one day a man walked up and said to me, "Father, I'm joining a monastery. I have a vehicle to give you for your work." This vehicle was a 4-wheel drive, which was just what I needed. I had never been offered a vehicle in my life, except when I needed it the most. I can't explain that. I think things are connected. There is the power of love, the power of God that is working in our world. This is an example of grace.

Another example occurred one night when I didn't have enough money to feed the kids at the ranch. The next day I had to go to San Francisco to give a retreat. I even thought of robbing the poor box or the candle box! I went to a meeting where a man said to me, "Here's some money for your work, Father." I didn't look at what he gave me; I just thanked him and put it in my pocket. Later, I saw that it was a hundred dollar bill. That had never happened to me except at the moment when I needed it the most. This is the power of God that is within this world. When we give it away, we get it back. This is grace.

God works through our human weakness and brokenness. Even as we reflect back on our darkest moments, it was the love within as well as cooperation with grace that eventually lifted us up and enabled us to keep going.

Saint Thomas Aquinas made the distinction between created grace and uncreated grace. Uncreated grace is the experience of God's Love within. Created grace is when we cooperate with grace. It comes via people, places and the infinite number of situations of life.

There are two reflections that have really helped me consciously locate my experience of God within. The first is this: I can recall a long list of people that I have hurt, messes that I have created, but, at the same time, I could tell you that all my life I have tried so hard to be good. I have always wanted to be a good person. That desire to be good comes from God's Love within. Even the very fact that you are reading this book is that desire to be good, a direct result of grace.

Many in my generation have two very powerful qualities. The first is that we are probably one of the most responsible generations in the history of mankind. The second is that we are the most guilt-prone. In fact we should have created a 12-step program for my generation called "Sorry Anonymous." Just reflect on how many times a day you find yourself apologizing to other people. I'm sure that all of you could do a good job of beating yourself up. How often do you give yourself credit for how hard you try to be good?

When I preach, sometimes I soar to ten, sometimes a seven, and occasionally the best I can do is a three. Each time, no matter what the results, I give my best effort. When we compliment ourselves, we are really giving praise to God because it is due to this divine call from His love within that gives us the power to be good.

The second reflection is that I have spent some very dark times in my life, times I felt abandoned, misunderstood, all alone. It was *eventually* that love within that gave me the strength to not only move on, but to grow from the painful experience. That's why I can look back at some of my most painful moments and be grateful. It is finding God's Love in the midst of my darkness that makes life a spiritual journey. If I were not to find God's Love, I would look at life as a series of events, some good, some bad without any sense of gratitude. One of Don's favorite sayings is that gratitude is the footprint of God.

Recently I visited some of my friends who had been to Medjugorje in Bosnia-Herzegovina (the former Yugoslavia). This is a place where there are reported Apparitions of Mary. They regularly send out a newspaper detailing messages from the most recent Apparitions. I looked at the headline of the paper and it stated: "Mary Says *Love the Love Within.*" Suddenly, everything became so simple. Loving the love within is loving God. Nurturing the love within is nurturing your relationship with God. Staying connected to that love within is centering prayer. Whenever we love Love, we love God because God is love.

Jesus' wisdom is not just good advice; it is Good News. It is not just a set of commands; it is an invitation to open our hearts to God's Love, to God's call. And with that call comes a new way of life. Many of the people of Jesus' day did not understand what the call was about and, even those who understood may have been confused about how it worked in their lives. The Kingdom of God is within. Remember, Jesus stated that the Kingdom does not come in a way as to be seen. But it can be felt!

When we are open to grace, we begin to see God in all the aspects of our lives as well as in each other.

During our most difficult times, God is especially present in our hearts. Eventually we may perceive our problems differently, but before that, our lives may have become unmanageable.

Jesus asked us to call this power of love within us *Father*. The book of Genesis explains that we were created in God's image. The word *image* does not mean statue or picture, but personality. We were created with the personality of God. We call this reality the soul.

We never know when moments of grace will happen. Jesus taught us this in the parable of the laborers. There was a man who hired workers at the fourth hour, the sixth hour, the eighth hour, and the twelfth hour. At the end of the day, he paid them all the same amount. Capitalists have real problems understanding this parable. What Jesus was saying was that it doesn't matter when we discover what life is all about. We can be twenty, forty, sixty, or eighty. What matters is that sometime during our lives we discover God's Love.

One day I was asked to perform a funeral. The family requested a rosary in the church the night before the funeral. This church was huge; it held over fifteen hundred people. I thought to myself that the rosary would be a lonely experience, just a few mourners in a huge church. Yet, when people lose a loved one, you do whatever they ask.

As I was walking over to the church that night to lead the rosary, I noticed that the parking lot was absolutely full. When I entered the church itself, I saw that it was overflowing. I had never seen so many people at a rosary. The next morning, when I arrived for the funeral, the parking lot was even more full than the night before. It looked like Christmas Eve; many cars were double parked or parked in the fire zone. When I walked into the church, it was packed. I had never seen such a funeral.

Normally, I would spend time getting to know the family of the deceased before a funeral, but my presence at this funeral was arranged at the last minute. Therefore, I wasn't able to speak personally about this man's life. I said some general things about God's Love and the meaning of the Resurrection. Afterwards I went to the family's home, and I heard this man's story. He had been the first black graduate of Arizona State University. Due to limited job opportunities because of his race, he had worked at the airport as a skycap for forty years. And all these people had come to his funeral to say thank you. More people had come to say "thank you and good-bye" to this man than had come to any funeral of any person I'd ever known. This man had held the power of God's Love inside him, a power greater than himself. He had been able to touch thousands of lives. Most of us have experienced that dropping off bags at the airport can be times of anxiety and confusion. How wonderful it must've been for travelers to encounter such a kind and helpful person.

Why did Jesus call this power of God's Love

within us "Father?" Whenever Jesus was in pain, he always went away to pray. He always went to God's Love inside to get his strength. Jesus was different from all of us. While we rarely go within ourselves to find strength, Jesus *always* went to God's Love within. Because He did, He experienced God's Love as *always* being present. Because God's Love was always present, it had to be unconditional.

Jesus realized that His ministry was to communicate how much God's Love is present within us. Jesus said, "There's so much love within; call that love *Father*." He could have said, mother, brother, sister, or friend. But in His culture, the love of the father to the family best-represented unconditional love. The Sacred Heart Devotion is a devotion to the Father within Jesus. The Immaculate Heart of Mary Devotion is about the Father within Mary. Jesus came to bring us to the kingdom within.

But here is the problem: Because of conditional love, we human beings never look within ourselves for answers. We do almost anything but go within ourselves to develop our personal relationship with God. We even substitute sacred things for God. Religion can, of course, assist our relationships with God. However, numerous people are attracted to a fundamentalism today. They seek a world that is black and white, full of absolutist ideas. This is happening because of all the changes in our world. Instead of having a faith that God is with them through their struggles, these people are controlled by fear. They substitute religion for their personal relationships with God. They are living according to fear instead of according to faith.

The scriptures are a wonderful gift from God, but too often we look for God in the scriptures instead of in our hearts. When we do that, the Bible becomes a substitute for our personal relationships with God. Catholic devotions, such as the devotions to Mary, are wonderful celebrations of God's Love. However, they cannot substitute for God's Love. They can be merely attempts to create God in our images, rather than let God transform our hearts from within.

The same phenomenon of substitution can happen in Twelve Step programs. We may turn the twelve steps or recovery into our gods, and never find personal relationships with God. This is co-dependency: trying to fill up the dark holes inside of us with people, places, or things. We can even become co-dependent on co-dependency! Every time there's a new book about co-dependency we have to read it. Every time there's another workshop we have to go to it.

On our wedding days, many of us think our spouses are going to make us happy. We've spent our lives watching romantic movies and listening to romantic music. So we've believed that one day we would each meet the right person, fall in love, have a wonderful wedding, and live happily ever after. But it doesn't work that way. In fact, if we haven't been disillusioned by our wedding day, we will be after we get married when we realize that our spouses are not gods.

Today, the new religion is "yuppieism." We believe that material things are going to make us happy. I believe all of us know in our hearts that we could live in ordinary houses, drive ordinary cars, and be happy if we have love in our lives. However, if we don't have love, there's not a house or a car fancy enough to satisfy us.

During one of my missions, some of the teenagers from that parish had gone to Mexico for a week to build houses for Habitat for Humanity. When they returned, they shared their experiences. Many of them could not believe that poor Mexican children could be happier than many well-off children in the United States. These poor Mexicans had large, loving, extended families, that were much more valuable to them than material possessions.

When Masters and Johnson did their famous study of human sexuality, they discovered that the greatest human need is the need to be loved. This need creates a spiritual dilemma for us. We want very much to belong, but we don't want to be vulnerable. In order to give of ourselves, we have to think we're special. And it is God's Love within us that can give us this gift of knowing our own preciousness. No one person can ever satisfy our need to be loved, yet this need is extraordinarily compelling, forceful, and powerful. In order to respond to this need to be loved, we have to surrender, which can only come from experiencing the desert. However, the problem—and this is the old Adam-and-Eve issue—is that most of us want to be gods. We want to be in charge, and we want to control people, places and things. We will go anywhere but within ourselves for answers. Therefore, we are unable to activate the power of God's Love within us. We never let God love us. Instead, we build walls around ourselves so that people can't know us as we really are.

When Jesus informed the Jewish religious leaders that they were all slaves to their religious practices, and to their rules and regulations, He also told them that He had come to set them free. The only process that can truly set us free is believing that God loves us; this love is what makes us so precious. When we live this, there is nothing in this world that can own us. Awakening to the experience of God's Love is what it means to be truly set free. God's Love is the only thing that can activate our souls, help us be vulnerable to others, and fulfill our need to love and be loved.

In the midst of our most difficult and painful times, we need especially to remember that God loves us as we are. God loves an unmade bed.

Chapter Eleven
POWERLESSNESS, SURRENDER, TRANSFORMATION

Let's pretend that God was up in the heavens looking down at His people, knowing that He had created them in His Love. Yet something had gone terribly wrong. People were trying to be gods themselves. They didn't accept how special they were as humans. But the biggest problem was that they were all trying to find their meaning elsewhere, never knowing that the answer was within. God needed to speak to his people. So Jesus Christ became the Word Made Flesh, God's word to his people. Jesus was God's word to us, a living example of the way He created us to be.

Jesus became the Word Made Flesh. His life was filled with pain and suffering. The religious leaders and teachers persecuted him. His apostles loved him, but found him difficult to understand. He did not have a family. He did not have a job. He did not have a place to lay His head. He caused pain for the people He loved. We call His mother Mary, the Queen of Sorrows. Why? Why was Jesus' life so painful? Because all of us have to go through the

Cross—to get to the Resurrection. All of us have to go through the Desert to get to the Promised Land. Why? Because conditional love causes us to look outside ourselves for meaning. To fill up the holes in our souls, we will go anywhere but within ourselves for answers. When these answers don't work anymore, we lose our meaning.

Jesus came for the broken, the sick, the elderly, the adulterous, and the alcoholic. Because of their pain, these people were open to His word, open to grace. He came to proclaim the Kingdom of God, the Kingdom of Love. He preached the Gospel. *Gospel* means Good News. Why was it called the Good News? Because it was about God's unconditional Love. The Jewish religion of Jesus' time had set up a system in which people earned God's Love only when they did what the religious leaders told them to do. If people obeyed their laws, contributed financially, and practiced their rituals, they received God's Love. So when Jesus taught the Good News, the Jewish Leaders decided to get rid of Jesus because he was leading the people away from them and taking away their power. So why did Jesus die? Because he preached and lived the Gospel, God's unconditional Love for us.

Every time we look upon the crucifix, it reminds us of how precious and special we are. Jesus gave new meaning to suffering and death. He taught us that through them we will find God's Love to lift us up. We are not alone in our suffering because God's Love is always with us.

If our sufferings have always brought new life, then when we are on our deathbeds, we know that physical death will bring us new life. Our journeys on Earth are experiences of death and resurrection, preparing us for the ultimate surrender. When we believe the Gospel, we receive the power to love, diminishing the fear of rejection, and we receive the power to live, diminishing the fear of death.

When we make external things our meaning, and they fail us, we experience pain and isolation. When we are desperate, we become more willing to listen to God's Love within us. This is when the Word made flesh can be heard in our lives. It's almost as if our need of God becomes clearer and louder when we're desperate. These times can become the most important moments of our spiritual journeys because these moments of pain and struggle allow us to be open to grace, the love within. That is when we begin to realize that what makes each of us precious is not our looks, our personality, what we do, or what we have . . . it is God's Love within us. When that begins to dawn on us, we know what it means to accept the Good News of Jesus Christ. That's what it means to be born again, to be reborn, to be baptized in the Holy Spirit, and to be saved. What are we saved from? We're saved from having to find our meaning outside ourselves. Jesus brings us to the Father. He said, "It's not those who say 'Lord, Lord' that shall enter my Kingdom, it's those that do the will of my Father." God's will is that we let God love us.

There are three key experiences of the desert or the cross during which the Word is made flesh in our lives. These experiences are common to most people during their journeys of faith. There is, first of all, the initial experience of feeling powerless, which is the spiritual awakening. Second, there is an intensified awareness of that awakening through the dark night of the soul. Finally, there is the letting go, which can only happen through the constant pain of trying to control the world. These are painful experiences, but they are also the times for which we may be most grateful.

For many years, I struggled with *Attention Deficit Disorder*. It affected me the most during my sleeping patterns. I had a very hard time shutting down my mind. At night I would wake up twenty to thirty times. Some nights, sleep was almost impossible. I discovered that when I had a few drinks, I could go to sleep. I thought that I had fallen asleep but, in reality, I had passed out. Rarely did I drink too much at parties. I never drank through the day. I never went on binges. So people did not know that I had a drinking problem.

I eventually had to face my drinking problem during the time I was a both a teacher and an administrator for a college program in Washington State. I brought education to a rural area. Paperwork, teacher evaluations, transcripts, and other forms, piled up on my desk. One week, they all came due at the same time; I was overwhelmed. A farmer had given me a huge jug of homemade wine. With all that paperwork due, I took the phone off the hook and, for the first time in my life, I drank for a whole week. I never felt so bad about myself. Prior to this occasion, I had always told myself that as long as I could work, I wasn't an alcoholic. I thought that if I could work, I was in control. That week, when I didn't work, I couldn't stop drinking.

That was the first time that I had experienced real powerlessness. Before then, I had always finished what I had started. That week was my first experience of being out of control.

I was so humble and vulnerable that I called my Dad, who was in San Francisco, and asked for his help. He immediately flew up to Spokane where I met him and, together, we drove the two-day trip home to San Francisco. He was so loving and caring that it helped me see that my problems could even be gifts. I never felt closer to my father than that moment. We were two suffering, vulnerable human beings. For the first time, I saw that my dad loved me like the father in the story of the Prodigal Son. My dad not only came towards me to embrace me, but he flew over a thousand miles to rescue me. It was an example of unconditional love.

The first time that we ever really experience our powerlessness, we have to ask ourselves the question: Is there a power greater than ourselves? Our quest for God becomes very real. I went to a Twelve Step program and admitted I was powerless. This was the beginning of my spiritual awakening.

For each of us, the spiritual journey begins when

we first experience powerlessness. Until this happens, we have no reason to invite God into our lives. We don't need God. For me, powerlessness was experienced with respect to alcohol. For parents, powerlessness can be experienced with respect to their teenagers. No matter how hard they try, no matter what they do, they can't make their children be a certain way. All they can do is give them to God.

Others of us may feel powerless with respect to our marriages. We can't make our marriages work, or we can't get our spouses into counseling. We feel we have no control. Or we might feel powerless to bring people back into our lives who have died, such as children, spouses, or parents.

The spiritual awakening makes us aware of our need for God. So we begin to search, to set different priorities, and to ask different questions, but we have not yet surrendered to God's Love. Something more has to happen.

The second stage of conversion happens after we have already begun our spiritual journeys. We have already gone from zero to one. This second stage is a deepening of the spiritual awakening. It happened to me after eight years of successfully working in a parish and utilizing a Twelve Step program. My superiors offered me a sabbatical. They said, "Tom, we want you take a whole year off to renew yourself and prepare yourself for the rest of your ministry." This sounded great. I thought I'd renew myself by reading books and going to seminars; I had a million different ideas.

I went to Montecito, California, where the Jesuits had a novitiate. It was on the coast just below Santa Barbara. It had avocado orchards, horse farms, rolling hills, and magnificent beaches. I had always dreamed of getting up in the morning without any obligations so this seemed like it would be a wonderful experience. It was the first time I could do whatever I wanted. I could read, walk by the ocean, and take leisurely naps.

This dream was short-lived, and soon it became the most miserable year of my life. I woke up each morning with an ache in my soul that lasted all day. I went to bed at night with the same ache. There was nothing I could do to take it away. Eventually I realized what was happening. When I didn't have my work, when I didn't have anybody to rescue, I was left with myself. I was all alone, and there wasn't anyone or anything there. All those lessons I had acquired I had applied to other people, but not to myself.

Being the oldest child in an alcoholic family, I had learned to take care of other people. I had looked after my father and the rest of the family. Then I had joined a helping profession. This happens to many people who grow up as rescuers in their family systems. They become nurses, teachers, or other members of the helping professions. My need to rescue was a way of living other people's feelings, of living in their skins. As a result, I never did anything for myself.

During my dark night of the soul, I came face to face with myself and arrived at the most significant decision I have ever made: *I am the most important person in my life.* That within myself is where I find God. At the time, this notion was very foreign to me, I was brought up to believe that, if I made myself the most important person in the world, then I would be exhibiting pride. I grew up fearing that I would get a big head. However, there is a major difference between being self-centered and centering on self. Being self-centered means having a dark hole inside of us, which causes us to use people, places, and things to try to fill up that emptiness. When we're self-centered, the more we get the more we want. We're never satisfied. In contrast, centering on self-means making ourselves the most important person. Then we can do things for others. We can't give others what we don't have. After coming to this realization, I made a list of all the services that I had done for those I had been trying to help. And I decided to start doing those things for myself.

When we travel in airplanes, we are given instructions on what to do in case of oxygen loss in the cabin. We are told to put oxygen masks on ourselves first, even if we have small children. If we don't, we cannot take care of them. This is a very good example of how we first need to do things for ourselves before we can help others.

Prior to my big decision, when I would take my "rescuee" to dinner, I would take them to the best restaurants I could afford. However, when I ate alone, I would stop at fast food places. I'd grab something to eat while driving. I believed that I didn't deserve anything better until I decided to make myself my own best friend. The first time I ever treated myself was in California, on Highway 5. I traveled it a lot. One of the best restaurants along that stretch of highway was Harris Ranch. It had its own beef and its own bakery. I ate a prawn cocktail, a spinach salad, a porterhouse steak, and two napoleons. I sat for a full hour and thoroughly enjoyed the meal. I was worth it.

When I was a child growing up in San Francisco, there was no such thing as a mall. When my mom would take us shopping, she'd take us downtown. We would go through all the department stores before she would decide where she wanted to buy particular items. As a result of this, I always hated to shop for clothes. In my early years as a Jesuit, I often received the clothes of the last person who had died. So I didn't have to purchase much. When that didn't happen anymore, I had to shop for myself. I usually grabbed the first thing I saw. Now I have changed.

I remember the day I decided I wanted to dress like a cowboy. I went into a famous store in Phoenix and bought a couple of cowboy shirts, a funny cowboy hat, and my first pair of boots. That night I went out with some friends. I was wearing my cowboy boots and thought I was seventeen-feet tall. I felt wonderful. Later, when I came home to the rectory, all the priests were asleep. But I could not get my boots off! So that first night, I slept with my boots on. Although it must've been a funny sight, the important point is that I did something for myself.

I had gone through my pain and reached the insight that where I meet God is in my relationship with myself. I had realized that, if I don't take care of myself, I don't have anything to give others. It had taken a dark night of the soul for me to come to that conclusion.

The dark night of the soul is almost indescribable. It can happen in many different ways, but what is common to all of them is the loss of ego and the emptying out of self-will. We all reach points of despair and deep depression where nothing in this world can give us anything but temporary satisfaction. This ache of the soul is constant and unyielding. It's an experience that I hope I never have to go through again. After the dark night of the soul, finding ourselves and becoming more aware of God within us, is tested by the struggles of life. It is during these times that our awareness will be deepened.

After I developed a friendship with myself on the physical level, such as visiting good restaurants and buying nice clothes, I deepened this process on a spiritual level by explicitly bringing God into my life and accepting the Good News of Jesus Christ.

As I look at my life today, I didn't really become a Christian until I was middle-aged. I was a Catholic all my life. I was a Jesuit since the age of seventeen. However, I did not make the Gospel the centerpiece of my life until I was forty-two years old. When I was a child, I believed that I was a good Christian by simply being a good Catholic. I was taught to be obedient: If I kept the rules, the rules would keep me.

Later in life, after I realized that the institutional church was not God, I became a humanist. My Gospel was just to be a good human being. I did not make the decision to become a Christian until I decided that the most important relationship in my life was with myself. I realized that if I could not apply the Gospel to myself, I could not really be a Christian.

Faith is a decision. It is a response to God's grace of love inside us. We are only going to make this decision when we make it, and nobody can make it for us. This notion is foreign to most Catholics. It's something that Protestants understand a lot better. The Catholic Church is a sacramental church, so it's easy for Catholics to believe that everything happens during sacraments. I thought that I became committed to the Gospel when I was in the seventh grade during confirmation or certainly on my ordination day. But faith isn't something that happens to us. We have to take adult responsibility for it. The decision to have faith is not a decision about what to eat for dinner tonight or where to travel on vacation. It is a decision of the heart. It is similar to the decisions we make when we choose the person we are going to be with for the rest of our lives.

I grounded my faith not in some God up in the sky, but in God's Love inside me, what Jesus called Father. This was the reality of loving God's Love within me. I suddenly realized that it was God's Love that made me so precious. God first loved me. That was the true beginning of my being a Christian. No matter how much scripture I knew, how many communions I had received, or how many devotions I had, it didn't mean much until I first believed I was precious because of God's Love. Before I had this conversion, I only saw the preciousness in others; I never saw it in myself.

Of course, just because I made a decision didn't mean I was going to live in a rose garden the rest of my life. I need to maintain conscious contact with God through prayer. I need to become willing on a daily basis to surrender to God's Love within me-to let go and let God. When I changed my attitude, I changed my thinking, and when I changed my experience of God, I changed. Today, I cannot remember the last time I beat myself up.

In fact, we know that God loves us when we believe that He does so while we're in messy situations. Because of Jesus' death and Resurrection, we know as Christians that God's Love is always with us. The times when we really need to know this are not when things are going our way, but when life seems dark and gloomy. These are the times that tell us whether our faith is real or not. Either we grow spiritually from these times of darkness or we become victims.

I once had a very humbling experience. Looking back at it today, it was also a very gratifying experience. One dark, rainy, Friday night in San Francisco, I had an appointment in a part of the city with very steep hills. I couldn't find a place to park; it was getting later by the minute. Finally I found a spot, but it involved parallel parking on a street that seemed almost vertical. Usually, I have difficulty parallel parking when I have fifty feet on each side of me. In fact, I'll go two blocks out of my way just to avoid having to back into a spot. So I said to myself, "It's either this or nothing." To make matters worse, it was a very narrow street. The other drivers had to wait for me to park in order to pass. Cars started lining up behind me. I didn't have a method to my parallel parking. I just pulled the wheel this way and that, hoping that magically my car would enter the parking place. The drivers waiting for me became impatient and started honking their horns. I panicked. Suddenly, instead of putting my foot on the brake, I hit the gas pedal and plowed into the car behind me. I had made room to park! I was not proud of doing that, and my insurance covered the damage to the other car, but I was proud that afterwards I didn't beat myself up. I reminded myself that this was the only accident I'd had in over forty years of driving. I said, "Tom, you've done a pretty good job. You just got panicky. You got fearful." I realized that day that the preciousness of being a child of God had penetrated my heart. I had treated myself as I would have treated a best friend.

As we improve our relationships with God, we change our relationships with other people. The Spirit of God works through us to others. When we accept the Gospel with our hearts, the Spirit of God's Love flows through us to those around us. This is called the Spirit of Christ, the Spirit of God's Love. Once we believe in our hearts that God loves us, we have to give the love away.

One day Jesus was teaching the crowd that we should love our neighbors as ourselves. A lawyer stood up and asked Jesus, "Then, who is my neighbor?" Jesus told them a parable that would challenge them. He said that a man was robbed and left to die. A priest came by, but did not notice the man because he was in too much of a hurry. To Jesus' listeners, the priest represented the highest level of society; he was the person who was deemed the most respectable. Next came a Levite, who represented the next highest level of society. He was also too busy to stop. Then came a lowly Samaritan. The Jewish people despised the Samaritans. In fact, they didn't even talk to them. So they must have been horrified when Jesus said that this Samaritan stopped and took care of this man, brought him to an inn, and paid all of his expenses until he got well. Jesus told his listeners that the Samaritan whom they despised was their neighbor.

Jesus' point was that it is only when we have hearts of love that we can treat even the least of our brothers and sisters with love. We can give love away when we have love in our hearts. If we allow Jesus to live in our hearts, we can express His presence in simple ways. We can show patience with others when we're driving, or let people with only a few items check out ahead of us in the supermarket. When we relate to other people the way we like to be treated, this treatment comes back to us tenfold. There is a Spirit of love that permeates our daily existence.

I cannot remember the last time I reprimanded someone for not meeting my expectations. At one time I had an iron fist in a silk glove. I knew how to make people feel guilty without them even knowing I was doing it. I could give a certain look or speak in a certain tone of the voice. Yet I never owned my actions. Now when people are down and out, the spirit of my actions is to show them how much they're loved. I'm there to lift them up, not to beat them up. I give away what's inside me. When we are transformed through our relationships with God, we change our relationships with one another. Conversion is all about inner transformation.

We all do some good things and we all do some

bad things. Good things happen to us and bad things happen to us. It is not the events that make us good or bad; it is whether or not we grow from them. Sin is not letting God love us. And not growing from experiences is not letting God love us.

St. John is called the disciple whom Jesus loved. It's not that Jesus didn't love the other apostles, but there was a soul relationship between Jesus and John. Thus John could write the gospel of love because he experienced Jesus' love in a very special way. In his gospel, John talks about only one *sin*; he doesn't talk about *sins*. For John, sin is not letting God love us. When we don't let God Love us, we live in darkness. And when we live in darkness, we beat ourselves up, we fill ourselves with guilt, and we want to disappear from the Earth. That's not letting God love us. John says that when we do God's will, we let God love us. Then we live in the light. When we live in the light, we believe that we are special and precious.

God's Love is with us when we make it through difficult times without becoming cynical or bitter. This love makes us more compassionate with others. It helps us to be honest with ourselves and more vulnerable with others. Many of us beat ourselves up over events that are in the past and we can't do anything to change. So we never grow from these situations. We don't learn from them. If we carry around guilts from the past, we're living in darkness. We haven't given them to God. When we don't forgive ourselves, we aren't letting God love us.

The spiritual journey begins with a few steps going from zero to one, but faith in the Father's Love continues to develop within us. On the spiritual journey we have to keep growing; our views on life must change.

A few years ago I made a second significant decision about my life. The realization began one day when I was preparing for the Sacrament of Reconciliation. I was making an examination of conscience. I suddenly realized that all the actions I was going to confess to the priest were not my sins. When I made an examination of conscience, I looked at all those things that proved I wasn't perfect. I confessed them to the priest. I wasn't telling him my sins; I was only informing him that I was human. It was then that I discovered that being an imperfect human being did not mean that I was sinful. It is not that we are human beings trying to be spiritual, but we are spiritual beings trying to be human. Spirituality is not about becoming perfect, it is about learning to let go. God can even love an unmade bed.

My real sin was wanting to be god. I wanted to be perfect. I wanted to be included in the Holy Trinity, the Father, the Son, the Holy Spirit, and Tom! Perfectionists always need to be controllers. When we are being perfectionists, we have images in our minds of what perfection is, and we spend the rest of our energy trying to control the world to match it. What is control, but wanting to be god? We try to be god to our children, our spouses, and everyone else.

As a child, I was taught in countless sermons to be perfect as my Heavenly Father is perfect. Scripture scholars say that the phrase *to be perfect* is an aorist verb tense that denotes *becoming* or *being* on a journey. It meant that I would become perfected, as my Heavenly Father is perfect. Therefore, it means *progress*, not *conclusion* or *perfection*. When I understood this in my heart, I made my second decision. I decided to resign from the Trinity and embrace my own humanness. I informed my family, the Jesuits, and my friends that what they saw was what they got. I was not going to change for anybody. The only thing I was going to change in my life was my need to be perfect. I had to be careful, though, that I didn't become imperfect perfectly.

God's Love shining through our humanness is the greatest gift we have to give. But we can't give it as a gift if we don't like it. How can we ever expect others to like us if we don't like ourselves? When I quit changing people and accepted them as they were, they enjoyed being around me much more. That was my conversion. When I reconnected with God, it helped me reconnect with others. When I understood that the greatest gift I had to give was God's Love shining through my humanness, I realized that the greatest gift others had to give me was God's Love shining through their humanness. "Where two or three are gathered in my name, I am present."

The initial experience on the spiritual journey is one of powerlessness. This is the entranceway to the journey of faith. The second experience is the deepening of faith through the dark night of the soul, when we make our relationships with ourselves the most important. Finally, there is the third important spiritual experience. In my own life, I call this experience, *my wife and six kids*.

All of us have to experience the reality that life is what happens while we're making other plans. There is the old saying, that if you want God to laugh, tell him your plans. In fact, if we were to write the scenario of our lives, we would never have put the cross in it; we would have never found God. As a result, we learn to let go, to go with the flow, to take each moment as it comes. Otherwise, we enter into some form of insanity.

I have lived on the road for seventeen years, almost forty weeks a year. I hate suitcases. I hate airports. I've known too many Chicago snowstorms. I've experienced lost luggage, and I've missed so many connections that I don't even dare count. Each week I've lived with strangers. I've slept for one week in a beautiful suite and the next week in a dark basement. I've gone weeks without a family meal. On the road I have had very little control.

Yet, I was also a control freak. I was God's right-hand man. There was a right way, a wrong way, and my way. Whenever I asked somebody to do something, they never quite did it my way. Of course, this proved to me that the only person who could do it right was me. I could've made the controller's hall of fame.

However, the road eventually taught me to let go. Now I try to live the Sacrament of the Moment. I go with the flow.

There is the old story about the family who got terribly upset because their only horse ran away. They were depressed and didn't think they would get over it for a long time. However, a week later the horse returned along with five other horses. Now the family was ecstatic and invited all their neighbors to a big celebration. But a few days later, one of their young sons, while trying to train one of the horses, fell off and broke his leg. Now the family was terribly upset because they needed the young son to work in the field collecting hay and grain. Again, they were very depressed for a few days. Then a government agent stopped by to enlist the son in the army. There was a war going on. However, since the son had a broken leg, he could not go to war. So the family celebrated.

The point of this story is the simple truth that we don't need to get too excited when things are going our way or too sad when things are going against us. They are both part of the flow of life.

Had I not learned to let go, I could never have continued my ministry. For me, as I mentioned before, living on the road is like having a wife and six kids. Life constantly bombards us with obligations. We either learn to let go or we go crazy. For the most part, I am grateful for my seventeen years on the road. Every day I wake up to try to do what I'm supposed to do and be where I'm supposed to be, and it usually works. It took me seventeen years to learn to surrender. That's just the way it was. Because I have acquired the ability to go with the flow, I experience a certain inner peace about life. This peace, which surpasses all understanding, is a real gift from a loving God. The Sacrament of the Moment is very simple. All I have to do is be where I'm supposed to be and do what I'm supposed to do because the only place where God exists is in the present moment. Yesterday is history and tomorrow is a mystery.

We can all relate to how wonderful we feel when someone listens to us as though we were the only persons who existed. But when they are listening to us, we are the most important people in the world because we are the ones they are with. On the other hand, we feel very lonely and angry when we're with people whose minds are preoccupied.

Recently, I was in a wonderful parish in Seattle where the people were very attentive to my needs. They kept asking me if I was satisfied. I thought to myself that I hadn't asked myself that question in years. Usually, I just show up every day, do what I'm supposed to do, be where I'm supposed to be, and everything works out. I used to spend more energy worrying about how I was doing than I spent actually doing things.

In Washington State, I worked with Native Americans. They taught me that we are not where our bodies are, but where our souls are. They said that the secret of life is bringing the body and soul into the same place. How wonderful it is when we feel this connection.

Recently I received a request from the YPO, the Young Presidents Organization. This is an organization of company presidents who have not yet reached the age of 50, have at least 50 employees, and whose companies have grossed over 10 million dollars. The Young Presidents Organization has programs for their families. I was asked to travel with a group to Nairobi, Africa on a safari to present talks and help bring out the spiritual experience of the trip. I had been to Canada and Mexico, but I had never been to Europe or any of the other continents. I've always loved animals, and one of my dreams, ever since I was a child, was to go on a safari. When the YPO told me about the safari, I was ecstatic. I told them I'd check my schedule and get right back to them.

I looked at my schedule and saw that there was a conflict. There was no other time for me to reschedule my original commitment. I began to think of excuses. Maybe I would need a hernia operation. Or maybe one of my relatives would be ill. I wanted some phony excuse to get out of doing what I was supposed to do. Then I heard those words: "Be where you're supposed to be; do what you're supposed to do." The Sacrament of the Moment. I called the people who had invited me on safari and said, "I'm sorry, but this year I can't do it. If you call again, I'd love to do it, as long as I have enough time to schedule it." If I had lied and had not done what I was supposed to do, I would've been miserable. It makes me angry when other people make commitments and then cancel them when something better comes along. It absolutely drives me crazy. So if I had done such a thing, I would have been very angry with myself.

The more we live the Gospel, the more it changes our lives. Jesus brings us to the Father, and the Spirit of the Father's Love works through us to others. That's how the Father, the Son, and the Holy Spirit are the three characteristics of the Trinity, our personal experience of God.

> Jesus began to teach them, saying: "Blessed are the poor in spirit, for theirs is the Kingdom of Heaven. Blessed are they who mourn for they will be comforted. Blessed are the meek for they will inherit the land. Blessed are they who hunger and thirst for righteousness, that they will be satisfied. Blessed are the merciful for they will be shown mercy. Blessed are the clean of heart for they will see God. Blessed are the peace-

makers for they will be called children of God. Blessed are they who are persecuted for the sake of righteousness for theirs is the Kingdom of Heaven."

                                                            —Matthew 5

Chapter Twelve
EMOTIONAL HONESTY

Jesus said, "Truly I say to you, unless you
are converted and become like children, you
will not enter the Kingdom of Heaven."
Matthew 18:3

I've often wondered about the above statement.
What is it about a child that we need to emulate if
we are to enter the Kingdom of Heaven? I believe
that children are honest about their feelings. They
don't judge, deny, rationalize, or attempt to ignore
their feelings. They've connected to the kingdom
within.

Don's son, Sammy, always tells the truth when it
comes to his feelings. Sammy doesn't hesitate to let
others know how he feels. He's very sensitive to his
feelings and is willing to share both his happiness
and sadness with others. Sammy doesn't censor his
emotions.

As an adult, I find it very difficult to be this vulnerable. I've accumulated a lifetime of angers,
guilts, and fears. It takes courage to be emotionally

honest. I believe that as we become emotionally honest, we begin to reverse the effects of conditional love. It truly is the most essential element of a spiritual life because it is the foundation of intimacy with God, others and ourselves.

As we have become disconnected from our feelings, we need to ask for God's help and grace. When I'm able to remember to be humble before God, I find the ability to respond to uncomfortable feelings especially those situations filled with uncertainty or ambiguity. God's Love provides the courage and the freedom to become honest about our feelings. When we reconnect with our Creator, it affects every facet of our lives. We are able to reconnect with our feelings and work towards emotional honesty. So, a step prior to achieving emotional honesty is to be humble when we reconnect with God. That's what it means to be Born Again of the Spirit.

You may be asking yourself, "Why should I take the time and risk the vulnerability to be emotionally honest? My life works pretty well as it is. Why rock the boat?" Maybe you should ask yourself another question, "Do I have all the intimacy I want?" If the answer is "no," the solution starts with humility and ends with emotionally honesty.

Intimacy as well as freedom are the fruits of emotional honesty. When we have emotionally honesty, we gain the freedom from fear and begin to establish healthy boundaries, based on authentic feelings. Many of us have very little experience of

boundaries because we were raised in environ-
ments full of conditional love; it is no surprise emotional honesty is a foreign concept for us.

My spirituality today guides me through my
deserts. When I look back at the messes in my life,
my deserts, they have started with emotional dishonesty. If we don't get honest about our feelings,
we will feel disconnected. We will be restless, irritable, and discontent. How do we break through the
wall of denial that we've used to protect ourselves
from being vulnerable?

We've used denial as a means of survival. Yet,
denying very uncomfortable circumstances in our
lives can have disastrous effects. For example, for
many years Don was a medic. On numerous occa-
sions, he was called to assist people with possible
heart attacks. He found that, although they were
experiencing excruciating crushing chest pain, they
were often able to convince themselves that they
were having indigestion.

In fact, what often happened in these circumstances, was that someone who loved and cared for
the individual, would dial 911 because they could
see how sick the other person was. But why did
those people actually having the chest pain so often
try to deny it? Isn't it because they were afraid and
did not want to be vulnerable? So they literally tried
not to feel their intense pain. Denial may be one of
the most powerful forces on earth.

The nature of denial is that we refuse to see

things as they really are. Where is the denial in your life? When Jesus said, "Where two or more are gathered in my name," he was saying "it's a *we* program." We can't see through our denial alone. Spirituality gives us the courage to be vulnerable, bringing others into our feelings, thus making intimacy possible.

Asking for help, being vulnerable, and bringing others into our secret worlds requires humility. Usually, it is pain that creates our humility. We become so uncomfortable with feelings that we reach out for help. For example, there have been many instances in the course of my relationship with Don where his honesty in regard to his struggles has spurred me on to face behaviors that I am trying to deny. But first, I had to have the humility to accept his observations. In healthy relationships, people are willing and able to confront each other's behavior.

When I felt myself becoming fascinated with the casinos, which are sprouting up all over America, and when the fascination became an obsession, my first response was denial. I did not want to question my priorities, even when I would go to a parish to do a mission, and the first thing I found myself doing was checking the telephone book to see if a casino was located nearby. It was not until Don expressed his feelings of concern that I was able to break through my denial. If Don had not been emotionally honest with me, and I had not had the humility to be open to his input, my behavior would have gone unchecked and would have led to a very painful desert.

This was not a one-way street. When you have the experience of emotional honesty in relationships, you can help one another. I recall that, in order for Don to accept and begin to work through his drug addiction, he first had to realize that he could not do it alone. Left to himself, without feedback from others, he could easily stay in denial. Just as Don had pointed out my potentially damaging behaviors, I was able to be emotionally honest with him regarding his denial. We were able to prevent the progression and make recovery possible. In fact, in many instances, Don and I, were able to see through our own delusions with the help of each other and break our veils of denial. Today we often hear about "tough love" and being honest with others. Even when emotional honesty creates conflict, it ultimately shows caring and allows more intimacy to enter the relationship.

Another step towards emotional honesty occurs when we become comfortable with our feelings, comfortable in our skins, and we stop judging them. We consider them important enough to share with others. Then wonderful things occur; miracles can happen because God enters into our relationships.

For most of us, when we become uncomfortable, we look for ways to escape. We look for any comfort zone. We may look to blame somebody because someone else must be responsible for our discomfort. I don't like to take responsibility for my own feelings unless they are positive.

Most of us have experienced instances in our marriages or relationships where we were hesitant to say something to the other person for fear of their reaction. We may have thought about it for days, weeks, or months. Then, our feelings would build and build until we were ready to explode. The secret to emotional honesty is to be willing to acknowledge our feelings when they are a three on a one to ten scale, instead of waiting until they reach ten.

One of the telltale signs of emotional honesty is whether or not we carry a lot of resentment. Whenever we ignore or deny our feelings long enough, there are consequences. Sometimes we convince ourselves that our feelings have reached a point of explosion only because of another person's behavior. We blame them, rather than taking responsibility for how *we* feel. They are not making us feel that way. In fact, someone else might respond totally differently to the same behavior. It might not bother someone else that the husband left his underwear on the bedroom floor. Yet we think, "If only that so and so had enough courtesy to pick up after himself." Or, "If only she had the sense to see that I had been working hard all day and all I want to do now is watch TV." We think that if the other person changed, we would then be fine. But how likely is it that the other person will change? Sometimes we think it will be different in our next marriage. Yet, that often turns out much like the previous one or more marriages. So what's the answer?

The answer is, first of all, to be emotionally honest with ourselves. We are responsible for our own feelings. Once we accept that and stop blaming, we take the first step towards emotional honesty and more intimacy in our relationships.

Children oftentimes deny reality then pretend, because they are powerless to do anything about it. We may take that same sense of powerless and carry it throughout our lives into adulthood. So, as adults, we respond to situations as if we are powerless. We may adjust our outlook to conform to how we would like reality to be, rather than being honest with ourselves. On the contrary, an emotionally mature and spiritually responsible adult, when faced with a choice of pleasing another or denying his feelings, chooses to be emotionally honest and risks the displeasure of another. Today I believe in the importance of the statement: "To thine own self, be true."

Give yourself permission to be emotionally honest, with others, and with God. You will invariably have increased intimacy in all your relationships.

Chapter Thirteen
GIVING GOD A GAP

And Jesus said to them, "If you want to come with me, you must forget yourself. Pick up your cross every day and follow me. If you want to save your life, you must lose it. But if you lose your life for my sake, you will save it. Will you gain anything if you win the whole world, but you lose yourself in the process?"

—*Luke 23*

We would like to show how grace becomes more apparent in our lives by introducing a new concept: Giving God a Gap. We need to discover that our feelings hold the key to maintaining conscious contact with God. The ability to respond to difficult situations with a spiritual solution is possible as we become spiritually responsible. This next chapter will formulize the process by presenting a methodology for a prayer life.

There are three factors to consider in understanding what it means to give God a gap. First of all, there is our personality, our feelings, our history, and our spirituality, that which makes us who we are. Secondly, life happens to us. We are constantly reacting to people, places, and things. We sometimes experience our emotional responses in intense powerful waves. They may cause great disruption in our behavior and with others: emotions such as fear, guilt, and anger. Thirdly, spirituality can give us the ability not to react immediately, but to give God a gap; thus, grace has an opportunity to work in our lives. Therefore, when we eventually do respond, God has had a chance to transform our hearts.

When we experience God in our feelings, in our grieving, our fears, our guilts, and our angers because these emotions are real and hard to deny or ignore due to their intensity. It takes willingness and honesty to admit that there is a difference between being emotional and being emotionally honest. The former takes courage!

There are two important points about feelings: They are neither right nor wrong, and they are temporary. I have intimacy with people who I trust enough to honestly share my feelings, to be emotionally honest. If I choose to share only the feelings *you* want me to have, then our relationship is limited by conditional love.

If we are uncomfortable with any of our feelings, anything that reminds us of those feelings makes us more uncomfortable; we want to change or get away from these situations. This causes isolation. For example, we all have experienced the death of a loved one. Why is that some people are able to experience the grieving process in contrast to those who won't allow themselves to be emotionally honest and vulnerable about their sadness and grief?

Don knew a fireman in Phoenix, Arizona who was killed in the line of duty. Brett Tarver was a big man at six-foot-five, and two-hundred-seventy pounds; yet he was a gentle giant. Brett was a husband and father of three as well as an inspiration to all who knew him.

During a large commercial fire, Brett got tangled up in the wires, and was unable to free himself. Although valiant efforts were made by his fellow firefighters, they were not able to rescue him. After his tragic death, the other members of the department felt a huge loss, and a certain amount of guilt about the inability to save him. What made this tragedy all the worse was that it was witnessed by an entire city live on television.

In the fire service, when someone dies in the line of duty, funerals are very elaborate. Three thousand people attended, including members of every public safety sector. Some at the funeral were publicly able to display their sadness and grief about this great loss, and began the healing process. Others remained uncomfortable, and unable to express their feelings of loss. When we are unable to process our grief, we may go for weeks, or even years, feeling isolated from others and ourselves. On the other hand, if we are willing to be vulnerable, and express our grief, we begin to heal. This kind of spiritual growth is the greatest gift we give to Brett or another's memory.

If I allow other people to see into me, or *into me see*, I have *intimacy*. However, as long as I deny my feelings, I create a separation between myself and my emotions, as well as myself and others. Yet, when I allow someone to see into me, we connect.

A woman recently came to me with this story. On Wednesday she had lost her only child, a son, in an automobile accident; then her husband suddenly died of a heart attack on Friday. In one week she had lost her family. When she finally went to her prayer meeting, two of her friends approached her and announced that she should be so happy because both her son and her husband were together with God in heaven. What a terribly insensitive comment. She may have eventually realized that, but first she had to go through a grieving process before she could give them to God.

If we can't express feelings of grief, we will bury them. I remember my own father's death. Being the oldest in the family, I had to make all the arrangements, call the funeral home, the cemetery, and plan the religious service. I realized that by being so responsible, I was paying no attention to my own feelings of grieving. In fact, a month later, I went on a hiking trip and spent a week just to experience and process the pain of losing my father.

Oftentimes, the grieving process can be a dark night of the soul. Although painful, it presents an opportunity for God's Grace in our lives. When we accept God's Grace, we receive the strength to move on.

When we are guilty how do we find God? It is healthy to feel guilt. It means we are sensitive; we are conscious of our own selfishness. When we are able to see our behavior from another's perspective we are practicing what it means to turn the other cheek and consider someone else's feelings. This is what it means to become spiritually conscious.

When I taught in high school, sometimes I would catch a student cheating. Frequently, the only reason he felt it was wrong was because he was caught. I remember thinking as I sensed his attitude, that he was not sorry for the infraction but that he was caught. That attitude would alarm me because it signaled that the boy did not have a conscience; he was disconnected. By denying his feelings, he was unable to consider the impact of his actions on others. In today's society, this scenario is repeated over and over again. This insensitivity is the social consequence of being emotionally dishonest.

None of us are perfect. We all hurt others and find ourselves in messes. We do some crazy things and, occasionally, even bad things. Hopefully, we feel guilty about them. That is healthy. It means we have a conscience. But what we do with guilt is either good or bad.

An interesting reflection for the reader would be

to ask himself when was the last time that he admitted he was wrong? When was the last time he could admit that he didn't know? In fact, oftentimes the way a man will admit he's wrong is that he won't talk about it anymore. Have you ever wondered why a man could drive around completely lost and never ask for directions? He would rather be lost than wrong. This is a great example of how pride blinds us when we need to be humble.

When we are emotionally honest, we give ourselves permission to be human and to ask for God's love and forgiveness. God's love and forgiveness is a gift; we don't earn it, we don't deserve it. But before we can accept it, we have to be willing to ask for it. It becomes possible to understand the power and importance of forgiveness when we have injured someone, and we experience the joy of being forgiven as opposed to being filled with guilt. I feel once we are able to experience such love we can grasp the importance of forgiving others. "The way we measure it out is the way it is measured back."

Seeing my part in almost any situation requires emotional honesty. This is precisely where repentance enters our spiritual journey. Repentance is the acknowledgement that we are sinners; that my self will vs. God's will was responsible for my fall from grace. Therefore, we need to ask our God for forgiveness. Then the way we receive this gift is by forgiving ourselves. In fact, a quick way to check my emotional honesty is to see if I am still blaming someone else for the mess.

When we give God a gap, we make a conscious effort to relax. Often, after some effort and practice, we can learn not to justify or manipulate, to forgo striking out at someone, not to be influenced solely by another's behavior, and perhaps become able to respond without an agenda. When the situation is too charged with emotion, too volatile, we can take some time out to give God a gap.

We have all heard of the example of the cup being full to the brim. If we want to add more water, we first have to empty some out. Similarly, in order for God to work in our lives, we have to have space in between arguments and resolution, fear and response, and anger and action. In order for this to be possible, we have to give God's Grace a "gap" in which to work in our lives. We have to look at our part in any given situation instead of blaming or denying. Then we pray for the openness to see the situation from another's perspective, to turn the other cheek. Finally, we ask for the willingness to help us when pride wants to take over.

Resentments are angers that are *re-sent* over and over. It can become a vicious cycle. When we see our part in situations where we have become angry and resentful, then we have the opportunity to break the cycle.

It is human to get angry. In fact, those of us who can't admit we are angry are probably nuttier than the rest. These people have probably spent much of their lives repressing and suppressing their anger. We are emotionally honest about our anger whenever we admit that anger is our issue no matter how justified we are in our anger. We will never feel better about life until we give our anger to God, giving God a gap. Then we can move on.

Giving God a gap means that, when I'm angry, I don't do anything that will add to the problem. If I were to do something in the midst of rage, I would only make a bad situation worse.

Let us look at some of the actions we may take which add to problems. First of all, there is the male tendency to have a short fuse. The man may convince himself that the reason he can get so angry is because of his wife or his children. He may feel it is very healthy to be able to let the anger go, to let go of that stress in his life. But, when he expresses his anger, he creates eggshells so that his wife and his children will behave in such a way as to avoid his anger. They may not tell him the truth about things, either by deliberately lying or by not saying anything, which is a lie of omission. They will only tell him what he wants to hear. The family becomes emotionally dishonest. When a man is able to be honest about his anger, to be honest about his part in a given situation, to repent versus resent, to look at things differently, or turn the other cheek, then he is able to give God a gap and process his anger. So, when he chooses to mention the situation to his wife or his children, he has brought it to God before he has shared it with his family.

One time Don had bought a rifle for his son. He spent a thousand dollars for it. His plan was that he was going to give the gun to his oldest son Ryan, but he first intended to ask his father to shoot it, then he was going to shoot it, and finally give it to his son. By the way all this was unbeknownst to his wife. In fact, all Kelly knew was that he bought the gun at a garage sale. As with many couples, Don and Kelly had an argument about money. Soon after this fight Don left town.

Shortly after returning from the trip, Don and his family visited a museum on Western art. Don noticed a picture and mentioned to his wife that his rifle would look very nice next to that picture. Kelly got that look on her face that told Don there was something wrong. He repeated the question with no response. He asked her, "Honey, what's the matter?" She told him that she had sold the gun at her own garage sale. She had been angry with him and sold the gun for fifty dollars.

When Don heard this, he was furious. He demanded that he and the family leave the museum immediately. At home, they yelled and screamed at each other. Don finally left the house to drive around, feeding his anger. Then Don called me and asked what he should do.

Don and I had recently been talking about Jesus' meaning of turning the other cheek. He had the wonderful insight that Jesus was not telling us to live in an abusive situation, or to allow ourselves to be hit again. But, he was saying that when we turn the other cheek, we see things from a different perspective. So, when someone gives us anger, we stop, give God a gap, process our anger, and give back love. The way we measure it out is the way it is measured back to us.

I reminded Don that he had had a wonderful insight about the teaching of Jesus, and that it was time to apply it. Don prayed over it, asked God to give him help, and he forgave Kelly. He even bought her a big, beautiful bouquet of flowers. This all happened on a Friday afternoon. If Don hadn't forgiven her, the weekend would've been a disaster. Instead, Don and Kelly were brought closer together, had a wonderful weekend, and were even laughing about it by Sunday.

A wonderful example of giving God a gap is writing the anger letters. This has been a very helpful tool in my spirituality. Sometimes, when I was angry with someone, I would sit down and write them a letter. When I'm angry, I want to tell people things. I just put it on paper. I don't worry about the swear words, the punctuation, or the spelling. I just let it all pour out. But I don't end the letter until it starts turning positive—if not towards the other person, at least towards myself. Instead of burying my anger, I'm processing it. I'm bringing it to God. Once I release that anger inside of me, then God's

Love within will start the healing process, and I will notice it in the writing. This is giving God a gap.

When I started writing these letters, I was astonished at how often I got angry each day, especially at the people I loved the most. Often, if I didn't deal with my anger during the day, I would wake up at two in the morning very angry. The more I would think about it, the angrier I would get. I trained myself to get up and write the person a letter until it turned positive. Then I could go back to sleep. About every six months, I would burn all these letters. That way, if I died in the middle of the night, people wouldn't find them. If they did, I'd have nobody at my funeral!

The point about writing these letters is that I took responsibility for my anger. I owned it. I did this in two ways. First of all, I dealt with my own feelings, rather than the behavior of the other person. The terrible cycle of anger is that when we are angry with someone, we stay fixated on his behavior and pay no attention to how angry his behavior caused us to feel.

I'm sure you know someone who has tried to own you, who has made you responsible to them rather than to yourself. When they were holding you hostage, your attention was on their behavior rather than on your feelings. We call this *enmeshment*. Notice how you paid no attention to how angry they made you feel. That is the exact problem with anger. We stay fixated on the other's behavior and take no responsibility for our own anger. There is no gap.

When we write these letters, we are separating our feelings from the behavior of the person with whom we're angry. So, now, we can talk about our feelings, rather than their behavior. Why is this so important? Because whenever you attack someone's behavior, no matter how wrong they may be, they will always become defensive.

If I'm married to you, and you're giving me the silent treatment, I would probably tell you that you're just like your mother, and that she liked to make your father miserable. In fact, your whole family is miserable. You would probably tell me that the worst mistake you ever made was to marry me. This exchange would turn out to be rather ugly. However, if I tell you that when you give me the silent treatment, I feel all alone in life, and I feel unloved, you are much more likely to listen, since you love me. Do not attack my behavior, but tell me how my behavior affected you. Talk about your feelings rather than my behavior. But you can only do that after you give God a gap. This emotionally honest communication is what builds community.

When we take the time to write, we are both becoming emotionally honest by taking responsibility for our own feelings, and we are giving God a chance to heal us.

When you write these letters, you never strike while the iron is hot. Whenever we express our anger when we're angry, we always make a bad situation worse. If we know we have to give God a gap when we're angry, we will allow the people in our lives to process their anger before we ever talk about it. That is why in families we should always have the rule that whenever anger comes into a family, we give God a gap, give God our angers, so that when we come together, we can make them positive.

One of the most emotionally dishonest statements that we can ever make is "I'm not angry, I'm just hurt." Notice, when I say that I am hurt, I am making you responsible for my misery. I am becoming a victim. Since I do not get angry, I never get mad. I just get even. That's why it is impossible to work through issues with someone who is hurt, because self-pity and being a victim is a sure setup for blaming someone else. The dishonesty is that whenever I am hurt, I am angry, and that is my issue. Until I release that anger, I can't feel better about life.

Another dishonest statement is to say: "I'm not angry; I'm just disappointed," or "What you do saddens me deeply." You can bet that anyone who disappoints or saddens me will make me angry. A common response to this type of anger is to withdraw or isolate. How many of us know families in which people no longer speak to each other. Their solution to anger is that you don't exist.

Today, when I find myself angry, I humble

myself, look at my part in the situation, begin to repent, and ask God for help, then I'm ready to share it with another. I have brought God into my emotions.

Fear is very healthy. Fear can protect us from unforeseen and dangerous situations. In fact, anyone who gets married today should be filled with fears. Imagine entering a process where there is a fifty percent failure rate. But, if a person can own his fear, it can motivate him to work on his marriage. This fear can motivate him to bring God into his marriage, to give God a gap during moments of tension.

Anyone with children today has to have fear. When, many years ago I finished my assignment as dean of discipline for a high school, I told myself I knew too much. In fact, if I had a daughter and she was going on a date, I would be sitting in the back seat with a shotgun. And that was in the 70s! Fear is very real. But if we are emotionally honest, we can accept that fear is our issue. Whenever we become afraid, we should do nothing. If we follow our immediate reaction, we will probably make a bad situation worse. We should give God a gap, bringing God into our fears, and then, when we have processed our fears, we can move on. This is what we mean when we talk about letting go and letting God. I'd like to share with you how I do that in my Prayer of Surrender.

This prayer confronts my fear, the most dangerous of all my emotions. The more I feed my fear, the larger it becomes, which indicates the lack of a spiritual program in my life. Conversely, the more faith I have, the less fear I have. When I am afraid, I pray that what I fear the most will happen—*if* it's meant to be. I name the fear. If I don't name it, and I try not to think about, I feed the fear because I give it so much energy. I face the fear down with faith. I'm not praying for it to happen, but if in the journey of life it does happen, I give it to God. I don't have a God who is up in the heavens trying to make life difficult for me. Life leads me into the desert; God leads me out. So, instead of my fear creating behavior that will cause turmoil, I give God a gap. I don't make situations worse. I bring my feelings and my fears to God first. My response to others is then based on faith, instead of fear.

It's time to ask some serious questions: How much are we controllers? How much do we try to control our spouses, our children, or the world around us? What makes us control? Fear. The more that fear runs our lives, the more controlling we are. However, when other people try to control us, especially our spouses, parents, and friends, don't we usually want to do the opposite of what they want? Don't we resist being controlled, either covertly or overtly? Don't we often become rebellious, passive-aggressive, or sarcastic?

My dad didn't have all the patience in the world. When he and my mom were getting ready to go on a trip, my dad would go out to the car, honk the horn a few times, and believe that this would make my mom hurry. In reaction to his impatience, she would clean the house for the fifth time, and check the bathrooms for the third time. The more he would try to make her hurry, the slower she would go. So they would usually begin their trip angry at each other. I'm a little bit savvier than my father. When I want my mom to hurry, I just sit down and slowly read the newspaper. The next thing I know, my mom is waiting for me in the car.

When I worked in a parish, we had a 6:15 a.m. Sunday mass. Many people went to that mass expecting to be able to leave quickly. In other words, they wanted a "quickie." I would start preaching and, a few minutes later, they would look at their watches right in front of me. Five minutes later, they'd shake their watches, right in front of me. I would just go on longer. In fact, I preached some of my longest sermons at the 6:15 mass.

When we try to control our loved ones, we can actually push them to do what we fear the most. If our children don't go to church and we think they should, and we try to make them feel guilty, they usually want to go to church even less. If one of our children has a boyfriend, girlfriend, or spouse we don't like, and we show our displeasure, he or she usually likes the partner even more.

If we believe that God's Love is with us, we believe that God's Love is with our children. The more we realize growth from our struggles, knowing that God is with us, the more we know that our children will go through similar struggles. If parents are grateful for their own pasts, they are very hopeful for their children. But if parents are bitter about the events of their pasts, they tend to want to protect their kids from going through difficult events.

I wonder how our modern generation of children will parent their own children. F. Scott Fitzgerald wrote about the Roaring Twenties as a time when people lived very shallow lives. But that decade was followed by the Depression—a time when people needed each other and discovered the power that was within them. The Depression helped create the generation that defeated Nazism. In fact, some of the old-time Jesuits told me that the best years for the Jesuit community were during the Depression, a time when people needed each other. If we have to go through our individual deserts to find God, society also has to go through the same experience. As the case may be, God is there to lift us up.

When there is an event like the Columbine massacre, people become more afraid for their children. Oftentimes this fear is transformed into controlling, overprotective behavior, which doesn't prepare our children to live in the real world. In times of fear, it is important for parents to honestly acknowledge their fears and replace them with faith.

Our relationship with our children is a journey. The best time to have children is not when they are

infants, not when they are little children, and certainly not when they are teenagers. When they are
in their twenties and thirties, each has to travel their
own journey. It usually is a very tumultuous period
in a person's life because they are discovering their
own truths. To go through this process when we are
young is enough; to go through it with our children
is insanity. Besides, we only get in the way. When
our children discover their own truths they come
back, not as children, but as adults. This is the best
time to be parents, because now we become friends
with our children.

So when our children are in the difficult part of
their journeys, we can pray that what we fear the
most will happen, if it is meant to be. When we do
this, it's very important that we also name the fear.
The result is faith that the same God who takes care
of us on our journeys is also there to look after our
children.

Another fear is the fear of abandonment. This
fear, which begins in childhood, can come from
physical, emotional, or spiritual abandonment. We
need our parents to love us, but we are not perfect.
When we get into our messes, they often make us
feel guiltier. This added guilt can come from the
silent treatment or just a glance of disapproval. We
are most vulnerable and most in need of love and
approval when we have failed and feel alone. So the
outside guilt is added to our own guilt and causes
us to feel like we have been abandoned just when
we need to be supported the most. Since there are

no such things as perfect parents, all of us have been affected by fear of abandonment to some degree.

Have you ever been in a relationship in which you felt something was bothering the other person, but they wouldn't talk about it? You could probably see it in their behavior. Yet, when you made yourself vulnerable and asked the other person what was wrong, they just said, "I'm fine." The effects of this all too frequent interaction between people can be devastating. The person who asks is often offended and distanced by the lack of intimacy in the relationship because the other person wouldn't allow themselves to be "seen into." In addition, the person asking the question may intuit the lack of trust and take it personally. Another aspect to this type of situation is that one person is not connected to their feelings, so there is denial. This leads to more isolation. Ultimately, to have intimacy we need to "see into" ourselves and allow others to see into us. Relationships are so fragile, so open to fear.

Our desire to be loved and accepted motivates us in our relationships with our peers, our spouses, our employers, and so on. We want people to like us; there is an accompanying fear of rejection. Because of this, we often try to become what others want us to be. This makes us uncomfortable in our own skins. We know we are not being authentic. Don likes to say, "Our insides need to match our outsides, and whenever they don't, we become restless, irritable, or discontent."

Whenever we feel that we are going to be

abandoned, we can pray the prayer of surrender. We can confront the fears with faith. We can build on our journey of faith. Father, if it's meant to be that this person will abandon me, let it be. I am praying that if this person does abandon me, my God will give me the strength to move on. But the miracle is that when I sincerely make this prayer and give my fear to God, I can be freed from the fear of abandonment. I can give this person his own space. Love grows when it is set free, but love dies when it is smothered. This is truly giving God a gap, so love can grow.

This prayer has been a special grace in Don's and my relationship. We both brought special gifts to our ministry. As a layperson, Don has had the experience of being married and being a father. In addition, Don has been gifted to see the big picture, to ask the deeper questions. I am a good storyteller and I can talk simply about complicated things. This chemistry has empowered our ministry from the beginning.

There have been times when I thought our graced friendship was over. We've endured serious illnesses, my gambling abuse, and Don's drug addiction. As with any relationship, if we are lacking a spiritual program, such trials can lead to alienation and a broken relationship. On the other hand, if we have a spirituality based on faith, more vulnerability and intimacy become possible

The human heart craves inner peace, especially during difficult times. There is but one requirement for this: real faith that God's Love is within us. Faith gives us the freedom to accept life on life's terms, to go with the flow. Otherwise, we spend our lives fighting reality. Our lives are then filled with stress.

This transformation from fear to faith can only happen if we pray. Otherwise, we're going to spend our lives running from one fear to another, like chickens with their heads cut off. We meet God in our fears. To our feelings of fear, He brings courage. To our feelings of guilt, He brings forgiveness. To our feelings of inadequacy, He brings confidence. All this happens when we have given God a gap in which His Grace can work miracles in our lives.

The Serenity Prayer

GOD, grant me the serenity
To accept the things
I cannot change,
Courage to change the
Things I can, and the
Wisdom to know the difference.

Living ONE DAY AT A TIME;
Enjoying one moment at a time;
Accepting hardship as the
Pathway to peace.

Taking, as He did, this
Sinful world as it is,
Not as I would have it.
Trusting that He will make
All things right if I
Surrender to His Will;

That I may be reasonably happy
In this life, and supremely
Happy with Him forever in
The next. Amen

Reinhold Neibuhr—1926

Part Four
PRAYER

Chapter Fourteen
CONSCIOUS CONTACT
THE IMPORTANCE OF PRAYER

Recently, after one of my sermons, a woman asked if I believed in hell. It took me a few days to reflect on her question and arrive at an answer. While I believe there is a hell, I also believe that, once we experience God's Love, hell is not an option because we know we're loved.

If we really believe that God loves us, this awareness has to affect how we look at ourselves. The medium within us that demonstrates this faith is our awareness of our own preciousness. When we place this awareness in the context of prayer, we call this our conscious contact with God. Jesus told us to pray always. When our own preciousness becomes part of our consciousness, we are in constant conscious contact with God.

Jesus wanted us to have this contact with God, our personal prayer life. In fact, when Jesus taught us the Our Father, he taught us the words as well as the attitudes we need to stay connected to the Father: *Our Father, who art in Heaven, hallowed be thy name. Thy kingdom come, thy will be done.* The words are *thy will*, not *my will*. We can remind ourselves of this when we're having bad days and things are not going our way.

Prayer allows us to stay connected to God's Love on a daily basis. To develop our spirituality and to find God in our feelings we need to pray. We should make it the most important activity we do throughout the day. When we don't make prayer a priority, we can't help but lose our conscious contact with God. Before we know it we are lost in our agenda.

We spend most of our lives living in our dramas, believing the greatest illusion, that we are in control. We move about, orchestrating our worlds according to our fears, thinking that we can change people and circumstances according to our wills. But it is only when we go apart and listen to our source, experiencing our conscious contact with God, that we can know that inner peace that can only come when we know we are loved. Then we can be truly comfortable in our own skins.

A good example of this is all the energy we spend preparing for Christmas: decorating our homes, buying gifts, and planning meals. It is only when we go apart and experience conscious contact with God's Love that we can appreciate what Christmas is really about: loving ourselves, loving our families, and loving our friends.

Therefore, the decision to pray is a result of our initial decision to let God love us. The result is developing a relationship with God. This commitment is manifested when we set our priorities. If we have a precious friendship, we should commit ourselves to nurturing it. If we take it for granted, we could lose it. When we nurture friendship, it grows and we have a stronger desire to enhance the relationship. It is much the same in our conscious contact with God. The more we pray, the more centered we become, and the more our lives are transformed. Over time, our conscious contact can develop in a way that becomes even more familiar. This is what it means when our faith calls us to become more Christ-like.

With Jesus, this conscious contact flowed like a huge river. For most of us, our conscious contact with God flows like a very small stream. Our fears, our angers, and our guilts build a big dam that prevents the water from flowing, at times reducing our connection to God to a mere trickle. As we mentioned earlier, a baby such as little Sammy comes into the world connected to God. He is not separate. As he encounters conditional love, silent praise, and all the fears that come from socialization, he begins to block the flow until he encounters the powerlessness, the desert, and the cross of life. He begins to thirst again for the love of God.

When we release the guilts, fears, and angers to a loving God, grace can then flow through us to others. The longer the water flows through the environment, the more it creates a natural, well-defined channel. In much the same way, our conscious contact with God gradually becomes more a part of ourselves.

We can experience this natural flow in relationships when we have allowed grace to enter our lives. We then see relationships as an opportunity to be of service. Instead of examining, changing, and controlling, we allow relationships to flow. When people become aware that grace is a gift given to them from a loving God, then they become stewards, being generous to others as God has been generous to them.

However, some people never gain the perspective that grace is a gift. These people assume that any positive situation in which they may find themselves in is solely the result of their own efforts. On the contrary, when people have a sense of humility they see themselves as stewards, and view their roles as being of service.

Jesus knew that the Father had given him complete power. He knew that he had come from God and was going to God. So he rose from the table, took off his outer garment and tied a towel around his waist. Then he poured water into a basin and began to wash the disciple's feet and dry them with the towel around his waist. He came to Simon Peter who said to him, 'Are you going to wash my feet, Lord?' Jesus answered him, 'You do not understand now what I am doing, but you will understand later.' Peter declared, 'Never, at any time, will you wash my feet.' 'If I don't wash your feet,' Jesus answered, 'you will never be my disciple.' Simon Peter answered, 'Do not wash only my feet then, wash my hands and head, too.' . . . After Jesus had washed their feet, he put his outer garment back on and returned to his place at the table. 'Do you understand what I have just done?' he asked. 'You call me teacher and Lord, and it is right that you do so, because that is what I am. I, your Lord and teacher, have just washed your feet. You then should wash one another's feet. I have set an example for you, so you will do just what I have done for you. I am telling you the truth. No slaves are greater than their master, and no messengers are greater than the one who sent them. Now that you know this truth, how happy you will be if you put it into practice.'

—*John 13*

We cannot really love till we first let God love us. God's grace works best with our cooperation. Faith is about making a decision; Prayer is also a decision. We are ready to pray when we're willing to say, "Thy will be done instead of my will be done." One of the most powerful examples of this willingness was Jesus' action before He was crucified. That night Jesus experienced the Agony in the Garden. He was filled with fear, yet He was willing to face the unthinkable if it was the Father's will. Many of us lose sight of the fact that Jesus asked His Father to take the cup of his upcoming crucifixion away from Him. Jesus wanted to forgo His agony. By example, He showed us how difficult it is to surrender. Remember that He was human in all things but sin.

Cardinal Bernadin was a recent example of the fear and anguish that precedes surrender. He was very honest about the pain and struggle he went through before he surrendered to the Father's love prior to his death from cancer. Such examples teach us that in no way should we ever minimize the pain that we may undergo before we are willing to surrender. Often this process takes a lifetime.

It's very important, when we are struggling with problems, that we quiet down and try to empty out the pressures of the day. Then we are truly available to listen to God.

When we pray, it is important that we know how to listen to God's response. Most of us prayed as children. Many times we prayed best when we were filled with fear. I can recall, as a child, being desperate. I would get on my knees and, boy, would I pray! When I needed God's mercy and help, I knew how to talk to God, but I had no idea how to listen.

Listening is a sacred act. When we listen in prayer, what is that we are hearing? Some people say it is the Spirit dwelling within or the voice of God. We're not having dialogues with God; we're listening for an inner presence. It is a certain inner peace. If we've been disturbed or upset about things, we can take a walk in the woods or along the beach, and we can feel this inner calmness. We begin to let go. This inner presence can, when we really listen, help us to hear what we need to hear.

When I started paying attention to my inner life, I found a need for prayer to stay connected. My first awareness of the process of listening to God occurred when I was directing a rehabilitation ranch for young adults recovering from drug addiction and alcoholism. I was responsible for raising funds, doing legal work, taking care of the boys, and helping them work through their problems.

One day I was worried about one of the teenagers who was having a difficult time. I had spent many hours and much energy working with him and didn't know what else to do. In frustration, I hiked up a mountain called Squaw Peak. It was a good, steep, hour's walk. As I walked up the mountain, I was very honest about my co-dependency and that I was taking care of everybody but myself. I was trying to manipulate people so I could control results. I said, Father, this is the real person I am. These are the real struggles I'm having. As I walked, a certain inner peace began coming to me. I had given God a gap. By the time I hiked down the mountain and got into my car, I was a totally different person than when I had approached that mountain.

As part of my spiritual journey, I focus every day

on what's happening inside of me-my fears, guilts, and angers. When I lived in Santa Barbara, I jogged by the ocean, getting in touch with my feelings and not letting them accumulate. I brought them to God. Today, as I've grown older, I take a daily walk for about an hour. That's when I pray and give God a gap.

Prayer gives us the ability to keep our feelings current. If we give God our guilts and let God forgive us, we don't carry them on to tomorrow. The next day, if we again feel guilty, the guilt is new, not old, so it is not tied into a whole system of old guilt. The same is true with fear. When we give God our fears and He transforms them by faith, then the next fear we experience is related only to the present and is not tied into a whole system of old fears. When we don't give our fears to God on a daily basis, they pile up inside of us. The same is true with anger. When we process our anger and let it go, then our current anger is not tied into a whole system of old anger.

Although this reality is never completely perfect, as we become more aware of God's Love, we become more honest with ourselves. Conscious contact gives us the courage to confront our issues. In our relationships with God, we can forgive ourselves because we believe we are loved. In much the same way, it is easier to believe we are forgiven by loved ones when we experience their love. When we know that God is with us, we know we are not alone and we take reality as it is. So, our faith in God's Love gives us the freedom to flow with life. Anger can be an even more difficult challenge, but our honesty in relationship with God will help us empty our hearts of resentments. We call this transformation the working of grace.

We can see the principle of staying current through an example on the physical level. Suppose I have an old knee injury that has never totally healed. If I then fall on that knee, my knee is not just impacted by that fall, but by all the previous times I've hurt it. However, if I go to a doctor and he rebuilds my knee so it's as good as new, then the next time I fall on it, I am not exacerbating any prior injury. I am only dealing with the current injury. God can rebuild us spiritually in much the same way. When we have prior guilts, fears, and angers, and we generate new ones, then those new guilts, fears, and angers are piled on top of the old ones. However, when we stay current with our feelings, any new guilts, fears, and angers can be processed in the moment.

Since all our relationships are mirrors of our connections with ourselves and with God, when we give God our feelings, we begin to listen to other people, especially their feelings. And as we really learn to listen to God speak in our lives, we learn to listen and appreciate God speaking in other people's lives.

When I was younger, I would to talk to God,

then I learned to talk to other people, but I never took the time or learned to listen to God or for that matter to listen to others. In fact, I never realized the difference between listening and hearing until I was well into my forties. I discovered that listening is a sacred act.

Just as we can't listen to others when we're reading the newspaper or watching television, we can't hear God speaking when we're distracted. We need to quiet ourselves to hear God speak to our hearts. This is why it is necessary to become centered and quiet on the inside. When we recognize the importance of listening to God, He empowers us. God gives us the strength to make decisions, to learn from things, or to appreciate our humanness. Trusting God gives us the freedom to let go of people we care about.

Jesus taught us to pray by example. Doing so means experiencing a conscious contact with God. Recently I performed a funeral for one of the dearest and sweetest women I've ever known. She had such a natural sense of God's Love for her and God's presence in others. She radiated this preciousness. She was almost always in prayer because she was connected with God's Love. Through prayer we live in the divine presence.

Jesus said, "When two or three are gathered in my name, I am present." When we pray, we allow God to enter into our relationships. When we listen, we create a new reality with a new perspective that includes the awareness of the presence of God.

This inner transformation is how our relationship with God impacts all of our relationships. The relationships we have with ourselves, our God, and others is a dynamic process in which all three continue interacting, always influencing each other. When we accept that God loves us, our hearts are transformed and we give this gift to others.

During marriage counseling, a wife will often say to her husband, "You're not there for me. You don't give me the kind of emotional support that I need in life." Many times this wife only wants her husband to listen to her and accept her. Her husband, rather than listening to her, is usually thinking about how he can fix her. When he tries to fix her, they get into a big fight because that's not what she wants. It's very simple. All she wants is for him to truly listen to her. Prayer makes this possible.

Two behaviors or attitudes that are often confused are acceptance and approval. We think when we accept someone, it is the same as approving of him or her. However, they are not the same. When we love unconditionally, we love the sinner and hate the sin. An example is Al-Anon, which is composed of friends and family of alcoholics. They may accept their alcoholic spouses, but not approve of their drinking behavior.

When I worked with high school students, I discovered that if I listened to their feelings, and if I tried to hear what was going on in their lives before I ever said anything, they respected what I had to say. I listened to them talk about their families. I asked them to describe their struggles. I encouraged them to divulge their feelings regarding their families, schools, and friends. Perhaps a student's parents had been through a messy divorce and he or she was very angry about it. Or perhaps the student was growing up in an alcoholic home so there was a lot of fear in his life. Or perhaps he had been physically or verbally abused the night before. I found that most students' problems were family problems.

Sometimes I had to punish the students severely, or even dismiss them. In general, they were much more respectful of what I had to say because I had taken the time to listen. By listening, I showed that I had accepted them. "When two or three are gathered in my name, I am present." Prayer makes love possible.

In dialogue with teenagers, I have often asked, "What is it that makes you most angry?" Their most common answer is, "When I am not listened to." I also think that it is one of the most common buttons for adults. So that when it is pushed, we get very angry. I know, in my own life, I get very angry when my family or friends do not take the time to listen before they judge me. In my ministry, I get very angry when people condemn what I say without ever hearing what I am really saying.

Listening is a spiritual issue that is rooted in our conscious contact with God. We can practice our listening, but it is ultimately an inside job. The ability to listen makes possible the working of God in our lives on two levels: we are open to God's will—*thy will be done*—and we are living in the moment—*give us our daily bread* where God is. God gives us everything we need just for right now. Jesus told us to look at the birds of the air and the lilies of the field and to see how they are taken care of. How much more precious are we? He told us not to worry about tomorrow or yesterday. Today has enough challenges.

Listening without an agenda in all its forms, between God and ourselves and between us and others, is always true prayer because it is ultimately rooted in our conscious contact as God works in our lives and the lives of others. When we truly listen, we allow God's presence in the moment.

Finally, in the Our Father we say the most important words we can ever say as Christians: *Forgive us our trespasses as we forgive those who trespass against us.* A large percentage of the teachings of Jesus are about the forgiveness of sins. Why is it that Jesus wants us to forgive? It is because God can't speak to hardened hearts. If we have a lot of resentment and bitterness in our hearts, these feelings take over our lives. This teaching reminds us of the old saying: A person who has resentments is like a person who thinks that, if he takes poison, somebody else will die.

When we forgive others, we give ourselves a gift. In the scriptures, Jesus taught that if we wish to pray at the temple, and we have conflicts with our brother and sister, we must first go seek peace. We must pursue reconciliation before we can worship. Then, when we come before God, we are at peace. Many people claim to be Christians, but when they arrive at this important teaching of Jesus, they develop spiritual amnesia.

God's Love transforms the attitudes discussed above. These happen in our life through our conscious contact with God. In addition, God's grace develops the tools of spirituality. We need these tools to change our attitudes, because spirituality is about changing our attitudes, which is all the result of grace. This is because our attitudes are transformed during prayer. Honesty, openness, and willingness are the three tools that are also given to us in prayer. When we practice these tools in prayer, we may also bring them to relationships.

The first tool of prayer is honesty with self. This tool was discussed earlier in our chapter on emotional honesty as mentioned before honesty does not come naturally to most of us. It is one of the hardest qualities in the world to develop; yet it is the most important. But we never get to perfect honesty.

An important sign of grace in my life is the fact that I am becoming more honest about my feelings, especially my pains. It wasn't that I didn't have these feelings before, but I didn't recognize them. I blamed others for them. Now, as I become more honest, I see the issues that I need to process and bring to God. The development and growth of my honesty can even give me the freedom from prayer to say that I'm wrong. And that is hard for a man.

God's unconditional love gives me the acceptance to bring my feelings into prayer. So I can feel my feelings more in prayer than at any other time. In my relationship with God is the time when I experience the most love. I can feel my tears, my emptiness, my despair, and my depression. It's interesting that a form of prayer that has come from this conscious contact is my freedom to talk honestly to myself. For a while, I thought I was becoming senile. But it's God's presence in my life. I can be walking down a corridor or driving a car and I will talk aloud to God, expressing my feelings towards others or what is inside of me. During these moments is when I'm most honest. This is an example of my daily conscious contact with a loving God.

The second tool of spirituality is openness. When we are open, we listen to our hearts. God speaks more through our hearts than through anything else in the world. If we really listen inside us, we know when we're around truths. We have to trust our intuition.

Jesus was a different kind of teacher. He was unlike the Pharisees. He had another kind of authority. He wanted us to find the source of truth in our own hearts. That's why He asked his disciples, "Who do you say that I am?" What Jesus said was true, not because he said it, but because it was true. He wasn't telling his listeners anything they didn't already know. He just wanted people to find the truth in their own hearts. When the crowd was ready to stone and condemn an adulteress, Jesus asked them to look first at their own sinfulness before they threw the first stone. He must have reached their hearts because they all walked away.

The third tool of spirituality is willingness. This tool involves asking ourselves: What we do we really want to do? Do we really want to pray? Taking the time to pray shows our willingness. Our desire itself to pray is a grace from God. This is the same willingness we show in relationships with friends, spouses, and children. We show that we love these people by wanting to be with them. Similarly, prayer is the desire to be with God. The more we have faith, the more we want to be with God and the more we pray. I asked my dad, "How have you changed as you've grown older?" He answered, "I pray a lot more" God was more real in his life, and the more my father knew that God was real, the more he was willing to pray and enter into relationship.

As we pray, we hear messages from our hearts, thoughts, and feelings. These messages vary depending on our openness. Then if we are willing to put the truths of these messages into action in our lives we may hear things we don't like. We may hear that we need to admit we're wrong. We may hear that we need to forgive. We may hear that we need to let go of fears. Are we willing to do what we hear? Are we willing to follow through? Are we willing to trust the Lord? Perhaps we may be willing to go to the Lord and let God speak in our lives, but are we willing to surrender? Are we willing to let go and let God? How much will our prayers be part of our spiritual journeys and our lives? It all depends upon our response to God's grace.

Spirituality is finding God in our feelings, the real people that we are. This is what happens during prayer when we give God a gap.

We find God in our feelings, our fears, our guilts, and our angers. And through grace we develop reactions to our reactions. For example, although our immediate response to a situation might be to react selfishly, through prayer we avoid reacting selfishly. Instead, we react with love. We can learn to react to life with God as the source of our actions rather than our own egos. Therefore, oftentimes when I say the Lord's Prayer, I do not say *deliver me from evil* but *deliver me from ego.*

A few years ago, I was giving a series of talks in Northern California and simultaneously giving a novena to some Jesuit novices in Los Angeles. My schedule involved flying to Northern California, preaching for three hours, then immediately flying back to Los Angeles for the novena. I was in my old pattern of over-promising and under-producing, and I felt I wasn't doing justice to the people either in Los Angeles or Northern California. I was very frustrated.

That day I arrived late in Northern California. I

hurried to the sacristy. There I met a fellow Jesuit who commented on the fact that I was running late. I apologized and began my sermon. During a break in my talk, somebody asked me if I was staying over for Easter. I said that I couldn't because I had to get back to Los Angeles. The same Jesuit priest I had met earlier loved to make jokes, often filled with little daggers. He kidded me, "Oh, you've got a Messiah complex. You have to do everything." I just absorbed his comment. I didn't say anything back, although I felt some anger inside me.

Later, as I was concluding my talk, I wished the people well and gave them a chance to applaud. They responded very warmly. I thought I was just giving them a chance to say "thank you." Afterward, the Jesuit priest commented, "Oh, you just wanted to get their approval." I hoped what he said wasn't completely true.

By the time I arrived at the plane, I was very uptight. I should have felt good after the talks since I had done something worthwhile. Yet I felt guilty about the possibility that I was over-promising. And I had anger toward the priest. To deal with my feelings, I pushed back the chair of the plane, relaxed, and brought God into all these experiences. I accepted that I was trying my best. I was just who I was. I was not a perfect person. I came to grips with the fact that I was a pretty neat person, even though I had human weaknesses. Maybe I was a neat person *because* I had human weaknesses.

I thought about the priest: how I had anger

toward him and he had anger toward me. Then I prayed for him. I prayed that he would be the best person he could be, and that he would grow and be a wonderful priest. Then I thought about all the people I loved, and I thanked God for them as gifts in my life. I thought how lucky I was to have such good friends. I took all my feelings and brought them to God.

When I don't take the time to bring my feelings to God, and give God a gap, and I don't own what's really inside of me, I get into moods. I get uptight and lose the present moment so that, rather than living in the present moment, I live in the past or the future. I either feel guilty about something in the past or anxious about something in the future. If I don't process my feelings on a daily basis, I lose touch with myself. That's the danger of getting very attached to the external world. That's when I lose myself, and the real meaning of my life.

My best form of prayer is simply bringing God into my real experience. I love the imagery of Jesus talking about the hair on our heads being numbered. Mothers and fathers love their children, but how many know how much hair is on their children's heads? In this teaching, Jesus tells us how much of God's Love is within us, how much God is taking care of us. This is what I think about and reflect upon when I get afraid. When I have fears, I try to turn them into faith. If I'm afraid, I have to surrender.

When I feel the guilt of acting against my

conscience, it is an opportunity to let God love me. I affirm the Good News when I forgive myself. I have gradually grasped the meaning of Jesus in a very personal way. As Jesus grew in his life, suffering his hurts, pains, and problems, He became one with the Father. The more he got in touch with God's Love, the more He understood his vocation, purpose, and mission. Similarly, as I have grown in my own life through my difficulties, I have become closer to the Father. The growth that has occurred through my suffering has brought me to depend on the Father's love and truth in my life. As I pray over the scriptures or reflect on the teachings, I see what it means to become more like Jesus.

It is important that we become aware of our own needs and our concerns. When we wake in the morning, the first things that come to our minds tell us a lot about where we are in our lives. If our first thoughts are about work that could indicate that our lives are about work. Our first thoughts involve the issues that God is inviting us to consider. So, when we awaken, our first thoughts point out the concerns that we can bring to prayer.

In my own life, I reserve special time for prayer. Whenever I neglect to bring God into my life early in the day, I lose touch with myself. Taking this special time is an absolute necessity. It really works, and it is easier now that it is a habit. Unless prayer is the most important thing in my day, something else will take its place. I make it a priority to face with the truths of my life, rather than escape into my systems of denial.

Lord, make me a channel of thy peace—that where there is hatred, I may bring love—that where there is wrong, I may bring the spirit of forgiveness—that where there is discord, I may bring harmony—that where there is error, I may bring truth—that where there is doubt, I may bring faith—that where there is despair, I may bring hope—that where there are shadows, I may bring light—that where there is sadness, I may bring joy. Lord, grant that I may seek rather to comfort than to be comforted—to understand, than to be understood—to love, than to be loved. For it is by self-forgetting that one finds. It is by forgiving that one is forgiven. It is by dying that one awakens to Eternal Life. Amen.

—Saint Francis of Assisi

Chapter Fifteen

OUR SPIRITUAL PROGRAM
A NEEDS LIST

The purpose of the needs list is to build a spiritual program that maintains as well as nurtures our conscious contact with a loving God. There are certain things we can do to enhance this relationship. So a spiritual program has two purposes: 1) the positive actions one takes to build up the relationship and 2) avoidance of the negative which tears down or impedes.

We are spiritual beings, yet we live in the physical; we live our spirituality in a material world that tends to pull us in all directions. We also have a tendency to believe that if we talk about something long enough, we're actually doing it. To counteract these tendencies, we must root our spirituality in very defined physical boundaries. This is our spiritual program: the practical, concrete manner by which we stay connected to our spiritual foundations. The approach of this spiritual program is simply to become more aware of our personal needs. If we believe that we have always been rooted in

God's Love, these needs will convey to us the means by which we stay connected to the source of love, God.

We must learn to distinguish between our needs and our wants. Our needs are requirements we must meet to maintain our spirituality and insure our connections with God. Our wants are desires we think will bring us happiness. We try to fulfill our wants externally, with people, places, and things.

There is an intrinsic connection between our needs and the people to whom we're attracted. The reason why we are so fascinated by others and eventually become dependent on them is they represent things we need to develop for our own wholeness. If we were already doing these things naturally, we wouldn't need to put them on our needs lists. Our attractions to others will produce the information about the work we have to do. These attractions are God's way of inviting us to grow in relationships, especially with ourselves.

One of the greatest obstacles to a healthy relationship is insecurity. Often, we use somebody else to fill up the hole. Then, when they do not produce as we wish, we punish them with the silent treatment, the guilt trip. Our music and our television shows frequently communicate that love is dependency. Dependency is basically using the other person to fill up the hole inside of ourselves. The more we become whole the healthier our relationships become. There are no games or no silent treatments. The great challenge of life then is learning to live with self rather than focusing on living with another.

I have been fascinated by free spirits, by people who love to just be because I have been so responsible. This need is the essence of my own needs list. In fact, the wisdom of this book has come from the gifts that Don and I have given each other. Eighteen years ago, he was a free spirit; back then I was ever so responsible. Now he is the president of Life's Journey, planning and organizing our new projects; I, however, am awaiting my next vacation.

Don taught me how to be a free spirit, and I taught him how to be more responsible. As we became more whole, we became less dependent on each other. Don developed a different needs list than mine. It included his need to become more responsible. Now, when he says he will do something, he needs to finish it. If he gives someone his word, he needs to keep his commitment. I was the opposite. I had to learn to let go, to not control everything. I had to realize that I didn't have to say yes to everybody. As long as Don and I each continue to work on the areas where we're lacking, our relationship as a whole continues to become stronger.

It is important to note the conflict that exists between men and women: specifically between women's emotions and men's need for freedom.

Men have a hard time figuring out women, and women have a hard time understanding men. There is usually nothing that upsets a man more than an emotional outburst by his wife. He may tell her she is just too emotional, and that if she had more control over her emotions, they would have a much better marriage. However, the real problem is that the man doesn't understand his own emotions, so he can never understand his wife's. Emotions are very temporary, but a man often reacts to a woman's emotions as if they are permanent.

In the reverse situation, a woman may feel threatened by her husband's personal life. She may think he has too much freedom to go and do whatever he wants. She may feel like a prisoner of the home or the relationship, waiting all day for a phone call. This type of conflict may never be resolved in a marriage if each person thinks the problem lies with his or her partner. In reality, if a marriage is going to grow, each partner needs to become a whole person. The man needs to develop his own emotional life, so this is where his needs list might be centered. At the same time, the woman needs to develop her own personal life and make her relationship with herself the most important, so this is where her needs list might be centered. As each becomes whole, their relationship becomes stronger.

The needs list of the spiritual program is composed of two important aspects: Our personal needs, which maintain our relationships with ourselves and God, and our relationship needs, which help build and maintain healthy relationships.

The Need to Pray

A Jesuit principle of education is *repetitio est mater studiorum*: repetition is the mother of learning. So we begin this section by reiterating what we have mentioned in the prior chapter. We do this because prayer is the means for our conscious contact with God which is the source of living the spiritual life. So we place prayer as our first need. Without it, none of the others will happen.

It is obvious that a primary personal need is to pray in order to stay connected to God. To be consistent, we must make prayer our highest priority.

Why is prayer so important? If we don't embrace our shadows, then we bury our feelings. These feelings later emerge in unhealthy ways. For example, if someone injures my feelings or my pride, and I choose to ignore my resentments, I could easily begin a sugar binge. Someone else might drink heavily to mask his anger. If our feelings are not processed and released, they stay in our bodies and come out in unhealthy ways.

Every morning when I awake, I determine when I'm going to take that special time to pray. I picture my activities for the day when I can be alone. If anyone later asks me to do something at that time, I say I'm already committed. It's the most important commitment I make that day.

We can process our feelings during prayer. For example, when we are grieving, we are emotionally processing things that we've lost. These losses can be as serious as the deaths of parents or loved ones or as minor as losing a credit card. Whenever we lose anything that has importance to us, we need to grieve.

It may seem strange that we have to consciously allow ourselves to feel pain. However, many of us still have voices from our youths telling us that it is wrong to have feelings. We may have been told to handle difficult life experiences like a man.

Don had a difficult experience with grieving after his first marriage ended in divorce. At that time, he and I had been working together for about seven years. He did not know how to ask for help, and I certainly didn't know what to do. He went through a lot of pain that manifested itself in very erratic behavior. It wasn't until years later that he realized he had never grieved the loss.

During prayer, we become aware and process our feelings, including our fears. How can we invite God to enter our fears if we don't name and acknowledge them? If our fear is not acknowledged and processed, it will make a home in our hearts. This can result in obsessions or compulsions that can become the dominant theme in our life.

If we're afraid of our feelings, it can be difficult for us to acknowledge and face our anger. One reason our anger is not resolved is that we stay focused on other people's behavior and neglect our own feelings. I would suggest, as an interesting exercise, something already mentioned, that we remember people, spouses, parents, friends, who have tried to hold us as hostages in the past. Whenever we failed or disappointed them, we immediately feared their reactions. We were so absorbed in their feelings that we ignored our own anger. Any people who place such expectations upon us will always make us very angry.

Other good examples of those who fear their own feelings are people who live in very dysfunctional situations. They might live with alcoholic husbands or spousal abusers. They are so focused on their spouses' behavior that they never notice how much anger they put into their own bodies. As this anger accumulates, they develop victim personas. They blame their misery on their spouses. They may live in terrible situations and their spouses may be guilty of horrible behavior, but they will never feel better about their lives until they release the anger. For the spouses of alcoholics, the Twelve Step program of Al Anon can be an important tool to recognize and process anger. Such a program can be used in conjunction with a daily personal time for prayer.

During my own prayers, I focus on staying emotionally honest. If God loves me without conditions, He gives me the freedom to be honest with myself and with others. If I don't take time to pray, to be honest with myself and process my feelings, my inclination is to blame others and make excuses. When I have the freedom to experience God's Love, I have the freedom to accept that I am wrong, that I've changed my mind, or that I don't know.

Therefore, every day I find a time to become centered. When I'm traveling, I often pray during my daily walk. When I return, I'm always much more serene because I have given God a gap and grace has received.

The Need for Nature

Nature is one of my best friends. I have a need to experience nature regularly. I believe that our culture, with its cities and urban jungles, can be depersonalizing. When we live in cities, drive in traffic jams, work in concrete buildings, and encounter many personas, we can lose our sense of humanity. Cities make us feel fragile and flawed, but nature makes us feel whole, wonderful, and precious. A society that has turned so many luxuries into necessities has also turned the necessity of nature into a luxury. We say we don't have time for nature, that we're too busy. Yet it is something that we need to feed our souls.

I love to combine my alone time in nature with my time with friends. My friends and I can have our time together and our time apart. Nature is a place we can be ourselves, not be preoccupied, and enjoy the beauty of the moment.

When we are troubled, perhaps we can walk along the ocean or hike in a beautiful forest. Then, perhaps, suddenly from within may come a serenity that makes our problems seem so small compared to the beauty of God's creation. Oftentimes the beauty of nature will bring us to peace, call us to be centered, and allow us to listen to the God of the gaps.

One of the greatest opportunities for a family is to enjoy nature as a family. Some of my best childhood memories were the family picnics. My dad and I would go fishing twice a month for stripped bass. We'd get up at four in the morning and spend the whole day together out on the boat. Those were some of my best memories as a boy, just my dad and me. I've known families who have even gone backpacking together. It's a time of family togetherness. I believe it is much healthier for a family to spend their Sunday exploring some new piece of nature, bicycle riding, or fishing together than watching Johnny play soccer.

We need to try new things to stay alive. All of us deserve sanctuaries in nature, places to go in times of trouble to listen to the voice of God, to give God a gap.

Me Day

Every week I try to have a "Me day". When I awake that day, I have no obligations. In suggesting such a day to others, I apologize to single parents and those who struggle to find a few moments of peace and quiet and those who do not have the leisure of the priesthood. However, we all need to adopt this concept as best we can in our own life situations.

It is important to have a *me* day with no obligations because I have a strong inclination to be a people pleaser, to always say yes so that people will like me. It is very easy for me to spend most of my time fulfilling obligations to others while neglecting my obligations to myself. When I have time without obligations to others, I discover the things I need to do in life. When I first began to spend this time with myself, there was tension. I felt bored and empty. But as I developed a personal life, I discovered that I enjoy doing many things with myself.

On my *me* day, I may watch a movie, read a novel, or telephone a friend. I may visit someone I haven't seen for a long time. I may hike in nature. My options are limitless. If I'm tired, I may take an extra nap. The important thing is that on the *me* day I do not know what I'm going to do until I arise.

When I first experienced a *me* day, I felt terribly guilty. I didn't think I deserved it. I would read *Newsweek* or *Time* magazine and feel guilty because I thought there were many other things I should be doing. I thought that time spent relaxing and doing nothing was a waste.

The very fact that we take time for ourselves is a statement in and of itself. We are making a commitment to being important to ourselves. If we don't take time with friends, we can't develop a friendship. And if we don't take time with ourselves, we can't develop a friendship with ourselves. It is important to become comfortable in our own skins.

As I evolved this me day, I moved from the initial stages of filling up my time with activities to the freedom of just being with myself. I had learned how to do things for others and for God. I had even learned how to do things for myself. But it took me a lot longer to learn how to *be*, to be with myself, to be with my God, and to be with other people. We are called *human beings*, not *human doers*.

The Need to Have Fun

As part of my spiritual program, I've discovered how to have fun. Life can seem so serious. So much of what I used to do, even when I watched the San Francisco 49ers, wasn't fun; it was a matter of life or death. Recently, Don and I were visiting a family, and we were all talking about serious situations in which we had been deceived by so-called friends or relatives. Everybody at our little gathering was so very serious. It was obvious that we were all taking our dramas too seriously. We were so absorbed in things we could never change.

I needed to learn how to play because it never came naturally. At forty years of age, I learned how to ski. I had skied once before in my life and, because I didn't do it perfectly the first time, I never did it again. There were many other things that I only did once for the same reason. I only went water skiing once or horseback riding once. I did not do these things to have fun, but to do them perfectly.

I'll never forget my first day skiing in Telluride, Colorado. My friends promised to help me ski, but deep down I knew I'd make excuses. In fact, the first day I had the "flu." The second day my friends practically pushed me out of the house. They measured me for boots and skis. I felt so awkward. I could not imagine how I could even walk, let alone ski with them. My legs were trembling. Then my companions hired a ski instructor, which was the best thing that ever happened. She was beautiful; my friends called her Bo, after Bo Derek. I spent the whole day with her. I would fall and she would pick me up. It was such a wonderful day. I enjoyed skiing and I enjoyed the relationship. Today I ski because I enjoy it and I have fun. I don't have to be the best anymore.

Until recently, I thought that my yearly back-packing trips were a great way of putting fun into my life. Then one of my friends challenged me. He said, "You know, whatever you do, you make it into work. Even when you go to nature, you go on an eighty-mile backpacking trip where it's all work. Why don't you go out in nature and just enjoy it?" He offered to teach me to fly fish. Then he tried to take me duck and pheasant hunting. He told me that I had to have fun with my friend, nature.

The Need for Exercise and Nutrition

On my own list is my need to treat my body as a temple. For many years I abused my body with alcohol, overeating, and overworking. I never realized I *was* a body; I thought I just *had* a body. It's important that we treat ourselves well in our forties and fifties, because that treatment may determine our health in our sixties, seventies, and eighties. This has become even truer as our life expectancies have expanded. It is important that our later years have quality.

After I stopped drinking, I faced a new addiction to sugar. I'm only now coming to discover how unhealthy sugar can be in my diet. If I have sugar in my system, I seem to have no control. So, with sugar, and me it's either all or nothing. Yet, I have more energy and feel better when I eliminate it.

I feel so much better when I eat right and exercise. I have much more life. It's easy for others to see if I'm taking care of this need. All they have to do is look at me. My weight speaks volumes. Also, when I eat right and exercise, I think right. When my life is not going well, I eat all the wrong things, quit exercising, and have no passion.

Exercise is very important. I have taken an hour walk daily for the last twenty years, and my health is generally good. This is also my program for keeping strong. It is important that we include strength training in our routines. Many elderly people have trouble climbing stairs or getting out of chairs because their muscles have become atrophied. Strength training is an important ingredient in preparing for our later years.

I also give myself the gift of massages. They help to remind me that I am a body. There are things we can all do to pamper ourselves.

The Need to Be Challenged

When I worked in a parish, I could be easily bored because so many things seemed the same. When I was bored, I didn't sleep well. I ate erratically. I had no passion for doing anything. I discovered that we need to continually do new and challenging things. We need to think new thoughts, read new books, and be open to new ideas. We need challenging projects, and we need to be around challenging people. Recently, I gave a retreat to high school students. I learned more from them than they did from me.

I love discussing things so that the truth may be known. In arguments, egos are involved so people want to be right. I hate arguments and love discussions. I especially like to discuss issues with people who think differently. I can learn things from them, and maybe they can learn from me. I seek the company of interesting people who can stimulate me intellectually. I don't want to always be around people who think like me. I often think, "The older I get, the less I know. I don't have all the answers; I just want to be able to ask the right questions."

If God bestows upon us the gift of a long life, we can continue to think new thoughts and do new things with challenging people in our later years. In the early part of my ministry, I was blessed to work with teenagers, who were definitely a challenge. Now that I don't work with them anymore, I have to guard against my inclination to judge members of the younger generation. What does that accomplish? Young people are living in a new world in a different way. Members of my generation must discover ways to connect with them.

A good example of generational bridging is my relationship with Don. Our ministry is the result of people in two different generations who not only could share their points of view with each other, but also could actually appreciate each other's perspective. In fact, this book would never have been written had Don and I not been open to one another.

Most younger people have different ways of looking at the world than I do. They give me opportunities to learn how to listen to them and see new perspectives. This is much better than sitting in a rocking chair, and talking about how bad the world has become, and remembering how I walked five miles in the snow to school.

As Jesuits, we know when we become old priests. It is when we start talking about the younger generation of priests as not having quite the right stuff. When I was younger, I thought that would never happen to me. But it is happening. So

I can either become ossified in my old way of thinking, or I can learn from younger people. I can see how they have things to say to me, and how I have things to say also. We can learn from each other.

The Need for Relationship with Others

When I reached my late thirties, I realized that there was nobody to love me the way I needed to be loved. I had a lot of good acquaintances, but I didn't have many good friends. While I was popular in the parish, I was still very lonely. The reason no one loved me the way I needed to be loved was because no one truly knew me.

People need to know us before they can love us. We've all experienced situations in which there were people we didn't like very much, such as a neighbors or co-workers. When these people revealed something personal about themselves, we then started to like them. A similar problem occurs in many marriages. A husband might believe that if he shares his vulnerabilities with his wife, his loneliness, fears, and anxieties, she will fall apart. So he plays the strong, silent type. His wife doesn't know him, so she can't really love him.

My problem was that I didn't let anybody know me until I really let God know me. I had to travel the journey of powerlessness, pass through the dark night of the soul, and suffer the pain of life before I let God love me. These experiences allowed me to be vulnerable with others. I discovered that the way we measure love out is the way love is going to be measured back to us. When we can give love, we will receive love. This is the very nature of love.

Following are the needs that must be fulfilled in myself and others in order to develop loving relationships.

The Need for Honesty

Just as honesty is most meaningful in our relationship with ourselves, it is crucial in our relationship with others. If we don't know whether others are telling us the truth, we can't have faith in them. Our words have to have meaning. If people are telling us what we want to hear, or they're hiding things from themselves, or they aren't connected with themselves, then we can't have relationships with them. As mentioned earlier, the most important quality in spouses is that they be honest with themselves.

We struggle in our relationships when we start hiding the truth. Once we tell that first lie, we need a million other lies to cover it up. Someone once said that the beautiful thing about telling the truth is that we never have to remember what we have said. Conversely, punishment for being a liar is that we can never trust the words of anybody else.

Believing in a God of love gives us the freedom and strength to tell the truth. Such a God also gives us the openness to accept other people in their weaknesses because they also have a God who loves them as they are.

We can make it easier for people to tell the truth. One of my mom's greatest teachings was that we should always walk in the other people's shoes before we judge them. When I was a child, my siblings and I would often come home from school complaining about teachers or fellow students. My mom would always caution, "How would you feel if you were that person?" She nurtured four very compassionate children. Again, we need to treat other people the way we would like to be treated.

It is very strongly advised that we find someone in our lives that we trust who can help us with our denials. All of us have blind spots and sometimes it takes a good friend, someone to whom we have given permission to challenge us, to help us let go of this denial. That is why people often have a spiritual director, or in the 12-step programs they have what are called sponsors.

The Need to Share Feelings

If I tell others that I feel only what they want me to feel, I'm not telling them the truth. If I am honest about myself, I have to be honest about my feelings. If others only like me when I exhibit certain feelings, they are expressing conditional love. I need to be with people who appreciate their own feelings and thus can treasure mine. If I say that I'm angry, afraid, or guilty, I want those feelings to be heard. I need to share them. They are not permanent. They simply communicate my inner struggles. There is a big difference between people listening to my feelings and people trying to fix me. When people listen to my feelings, I am accepted. When they try to fix me, I feel controlled. It's important to emphasize, as mentioned earlier, that acceptance is not approval. I may not approve of your anger, but I can accept it.

As noted earlier, a wife might say that she needs to be emotionally supported by her husband. She really wants to be heard by a husband without an agenda. If he listens to her, he shows that he accepts her. If instead he tries to fix her, he's listening only to himself, and a fight will ensue. Listening is a sacred act. In relationships, sharing our feelings must go hand-in-hand with having partners and friends who listen to us.

In order to grow, most relationships need to develop positive programs to process their angers. Whenever anger emerges, there is a reason. There is either too much control or too much dependency. There is either too much "I" or too much "we." We become angry when others try to control us, and we may do the opposite of what they want us to do. Alternatively, when people want to depend on us too much, and smother us, we want to run the other way as fast as we can. When we get angry, our anger is speaking to us about our relationships. In much the same way, when a temperature gauge indicates that an engine is overheating, we must stop the car or we will burn up the engine. In the same way, we must pay attention to our anger before it destroys our relationships.

There is an important fundamental principle: We can't change anybody. As noted earlier, the greatest illusion in the world is that we're in control. Usually, when we fail at things, we learn from our failures. However, we often attempt to change other people over and over again without success, never learning that it can't be done. In fact, one of my greatest hopes is that some day I will meet a person who has successfully been able to change someone. Then I will happily return to my old habit of trying to change people! But I have yet to find that person.

Because we can never change anyone, blaming them can never succeed. Whenever we attack them, they become defensive. So blaming and attacking people usually makes things worse. Anger is not about blaming, it is about changing ourselves. Whenever anger comes into relationships, we need to stop and reflect on the real issue: Is there too much control, or too much dependency? This can give us insights on how we can change to make the relationships better.

We have developed a four-step process that helps me grow from my anger. The first step is to reflect on whether there is too much *I* or too much *we*. The second step is to inform the person that I am going to change. The third step is to be aware of my negative forms of anger, and not to let them control my behavior. The fourth step is always beware of the other person's countermoves. I'm doing this for me to grow; I'm not doing this so that someone else will change.

Don's and my relationship is a good example of what I'm talking about. Don, as has been mentioned, was a free spirit while I was "Mr. Responsibility." We'd often argue because I didn't think he was doing enough, and he thought I was controlling everything. I'm one of those people where there is a right way, a wrong way, and my way. Whenever I delegate authority to others, they don't quite do it my way, which just proves that the only one who can do it right is me. When people work for someone like me, they think if the "old man" wants to do everything, we'll let him do everything.

I told Don that I was going to change. I told him that I wasn't going to blame anymore. I was going to cut my work in half, and he had to pick up the slack. Today, as I mentioned, we have become very balanced in our relationship. Don works a lot more, and I relax a lot more.

I did this by instituting the first step and realizing that there was too much "I" in our company. I realized that there had to be more "we". In step two, I informed Don that I was going to change. In the third step, I had to be careful that I didn't let my passive-aggressive tendencies to be angry sabotage the process. I had to recognize that, when I behaved that way, I was only making a bad situation worse.

In other words, I had to be emotionally honest. In the fourth step, I had to make sure that I knew I was doing this for me, and I was not doing it to get a reaction from Don so he would do more. Otherwise, he would see my actions as a manipulation.

By creating positive programs to face anger, we can learn to listen without fear of anger. These expressions of anger then become opportunities for growth. If we can process our anger and make it positive, we can make all our feelings in relationships positive.

The Need for Communication

Communication involves something other than just feelings. It involves being able to share our stories. To truly communicate, we need to be ourselves with other people. We need to be persons rather than personas. When we share our experiences, our hopes and dreams and lives, people get to know us; and then they can love us. This happens when friends talk about subjects that are beyond the superficial. Men can talk about more than sports and politics; they can talk about their hearts, and what is happening to them as persons. These are their stories. Again, if people don't know us, they can't love us.

Let's say a student has an important assignment. But at the same time her mother is very sick and needs her help, so she doesn't have time to finish it. Or maybe her boyfriend calls and ends a long relationship, so she is emotionally distraught and can't concentrate. When she has to explain her situation to her teacher, it makes a big difference whether the teacher is a person or a persona.

Recently, I was privileged to take a walk with a much admired football player. He talked about his high school football coach, who was like a father to all the players. The athlete described how much the coach loved the players and how much the players loved him. The coach was a person, not a persona, so the players could tell their stories to him. They could go to him and be real, and they would be accepted. Communication is so important in relationships. We need to be able to communicate our stories to each other.

One of the greatest gifts in my life was the friendship I had with my dad. For much of our lives, our relationship was strictly father-son. He pointed out the times I ate too fast or was a little heavy. He even taught me how to drive over and over again, as if I remained fifteen years old. He was also very Irish, so it was difficult for him to share his story or to be personal about anything. I had a similar problem. As a second-generation Irishman, when anything approached the personal, I wanted to shut down. This was true even with all my education and experience.

One day my dad began to share his story. He talked about his childhood. He described how his dad abandoned him when he was six months old and how difficult it was to grow up without a father. He related how, during the Depression, he worked two jobs in grade school to put food on the table. When my dad shared his story, I began to know him and love him on a deeper level. I came to discover that many of his conflicts were similar to mine. The wisdom he had gained from his struggles was the same wisdom I needed to learn. In fact, when my dad told me his story, he not only helped me know and love him, he helped me know my own story.

The Need to Trust Each Other with Our Weaknesses

It is during moments of weakness that we deepen our friendships. When we injure other people, we feel terrible. However, the future of our relationships with people is determined by whether they make us feel guilty or help us to grow. This is when we build either bridges of friendship or walls of separation. It is when we decide whether we can trust these other people or not. There are many adults in their forties who are open with their friends but are still afraid of their parents' reactions.

The truths of our shadows become apparent in all our important relationships. Our brokenness brings us together. It is during moments of tragedy that real bonds of love are forged. Just as in our relationships with God, in all our important relationships our brokenness, our weaknesses, and our sinfulness become gifts. Through them, we learn to know and love each other on deeper levels. We would not have the ability to love another person, as they are if we didn't have our own weaknesses and brokenness. Only when we discover how precious we are in our own brokenness can we discover how precious others are in their brokenness. Thus, our shadows become our strengths.

It is in our own brokenness that we find God's Love and forgiveness. Our weaknesses give us the power to love others as they are. Letting God love us in our brokenness sets us free and gives us the force to create community. "My one commandment is that you love one another as I have loved you."

Telling the truth, being open with our feelings, and communicating are all interconnected as we grow in our relationships. Furthermore, our relationships with God, our relationships with ourselves, and our relationships with others are constantly interrelated. We can never separate them. If we are alive in one relationship, we are alive in another. If we are weak in one relationship, we are weak in others.

Therefore, the keys to our relationships with others are our relationships with ourselves and with God. We must be vulnerable to God's Love before we can give it away to others. When we have the strength of God's presence, we have more freedom to share ourselves because rejection by others does not have such dire consequences. We have an inner

strength that comes from God rather than from
others. We share our love with others rather than
trying to find it in others.

The *interconnectedness* of our relationships with
God, ourselves, and others supports the importance
of prayer. A time of prayer is a special time when
we can discover the love to forgive, the inner work
of taking responsibility for our feelings, and the
process of letting God forgive us. Prayer is the ter-
minal where all our relationships come together.

In Conclusion

In Western thought, there are traditionally four
aspects of love. All four have to be present in a relationship, but they vary in degree, depending on the
type of relationship.

The first aspect of love is physical attraction or
lust. This is the invitation and the motivation to
love. Infatuation normally lasts about eighteen
months, but often couples marry during this
stage. Lust or physical attraction is not really love,
because love is not primarily emotions. Love is
certainly not dependency. But infatuation can be
the beginning stage of the journey of love. For that
reason, it's an essential part of love. There is
something I've noticed during my counseling of
couples: If the people never go through the infatuation stage, and they marry just to please their
parents or because they feel obligated, they often
are unable to hold their marriage together if they

later run into problems. Yet if two people are in love, and they later encounter difficulties in their marriage, they can usually mend their love and their relationship if they have the willingness.

We are not solely physical beings. We are also spiritual. So there is a spiritual component to physical attraction. People who possess what we lack often fascinate us. It is said that opposites attract.

The second aspect of love is passion or Eros. This is the excitement of being together after having been apart. A lover may drive two hours through a blinding snowstorm to spend fifteen minutes with the person he or she loves; the passion makes the drive seem short. This passion can also manifest itself as the excitement of a young child when he sees dad come home from work, or the tears of a father when his son scores a winning touchdown, or the love of a mother when she watches her youngest daughter get married. Passion is evident when we visit with soul brothers or sisters whom we haven't seen for years: We talk with them as if we had just seen them yesterday.

The third aspect of love is friendship. Friends are able to laugh and play together. They have periods in their relationships without problems, and they can take long hikes together without having to talk. Whereas the first two aspects of love, lust and passion, are usually the chemistry in relationships, friendship is something that takes time and effort. For friendship to grow, it is helpful for people to do things together, such as play sports or travel. We all know the difference between friends and acquaintances.

The fourth aspect of love is called *caritas* or *agape*, the Christian love that comes from a loving God. This love is the foundation of the previous three. If this love is missing, the other three will wither and die.

> When the Son of Man comes as king, and all the angels with him, He will sit on his royal throne and the people of all nations will be gathered for him and he will divide them into two groups, just as a shepherd separates the sheep from the goats. He will put the righteous people at his right and the others at the left, and the king will say to the people at the right, "Come, you that are blessed by my Father! Come and possess the kingdom that has been prepared for you ever since the creation of the world. I was hungry and you fed me, thirsty and you gave me drink; I was a stranger and you received me in your homes. I was naked and you clothed me. I was sick and you took care of me, in prison and you visited me." The righteous will then answer him, "When, Lord, did we see you hungry and feed you, or thirsty and give you drink? When did we ever see you as a stranger and welcome you into our homes, or naked and clothe you?

When did we ever see you sick or in prison, and visit you?" And the king will reply, "I tell you, whenever you did this for one of the least important of these brothers of mine, you did it for me!" Then He will say to those on his left, "Away from me you that are under God's curse! Away to the eternal fire which has been prepared for the devil and his angels! I was hungry but you would not feed me, thirsty but you would not give me drink. I was a stranger but you would not welcome me into your homes. I was naked but you would not clothe me. I was sick and in prison, but you would not take care of me." Then they will answer Him, "When, Lord, did we ever see you hungry or thirsty or a stranger or naked or sick or in prison and we would not help you?" And the king will reply, "I tell you whenever you refuse to help one of the least important ones, you refuse to help me." These then will be sent off to eternal punishment, and the righteous will go to eternal life.   —*Matthew 25*

This is the only place in the Gospel where Jesus defines the content of our final judgment. When we believe as the Gospel teaches us that God loves us without any conditions, we enter Jesus' Kingdom of Love. We demonstrate this love in the way we treat the least of our brothers. This is a common precept of all religions: We must treat others the way we would like to be treated.

Jesus' wisdom is not just good advice; it is Good News. It is not a set of laws and commands; it is an invitation to open your heart to God's Love and God's call. With that loving call comes a new strength, a new motivation. Jesus came to call us to a whole new way of life. His wisdom tells us how we can be part of it.

A Final Reflection from Don

I introduced this book with Father Tom. I would now like to leave you with a few final thoughts.

Becoming aware of grace in my life has been an awesome experience. For me, grace has often come in the form of other people. When I have been most broken, they have been there to love and lift me up. They taught me much about God's Love. Another teacher has been many very painful and humbling experiences. I have come to see these events as special moments of grace. They have led me to what it means to surrender.

It was most necessary for me to experience shame with all its ugliness, my resentments that filled me with rage, and the fears that everything I held dear could be lost. I found God in my feelings. Most of my life I had been more concerned about the feelings of others, with little or no regard for my own. When I became conscious of my feelings, I began to be conscious of God working in my life. I would like to end with a letter that I wrote for my children:

Dear Children,

Today there exists isolation, loneliness and more fear than ever before. People can spend all day in front of a computer, drive home, open the garage door with a clicker, and avoid any meaningful human interaction. Many of us feel trapped in an economic system that pays little attention to our spiritual needs.

We cannot escape the consequences that result from a lack of spirituality. We reap what we sow. With the breakdown of the family, the dismissal of religion, and the desire for immediate gratification, we have created a void that only a relationship with God will fill. You children are going to encounter many of the situations we've discussed in this book. In the midst of it all, you may find yourself asking the question I asked: What is it all about and is love really possible? That's what this book has tried to convey. We often find the answer to that question by passing through the door of suffering and brokenness. That's often the only way we become aware of God.

You may understand God differently than I, but what is important is that you know that there is a power greater than yourself. Even in the darkest of hours, you are never alone. But, remember what Jesus tells us, The Kingdom is within. The greatest gift we give to those we love is to share ourselves. Remember to listen to others, to give them time. I hope you realize that people are more important than things. What is in your heart is more important than the world of appearances. The more that you build a strong spiritual foundation when you're young, the less fearful your journey will be.

In the not too distant future, there will be a knock at your door. When you open it, you may find the unwelcome guests of fear, pain, or suffering. It may come in the form of economic suffering, failed relationships, or physical or emotional illnesses. I pray that you will have the spiritual strength to walk through your deserts and to turn these difficulties into opportunities to grow.

Finally, one of the best ways I have discovered to stay connected to God is to be of service to others. We receive love whenever we give it away. It is important to treat others as we would like to be treated. I know love is forever and everything else fades away.

My prayer for you is to stay close to the love inside and cherish love wherever you may find it.

Love,

Dad

Life's Journey Catalog of CD's and DVD's

Life's Journey is proud to present this list of available materials.

Suggested tax-deductible donations for audiotapes are $35 per series of 4 CD's. For a complete list of materials that we offer, please contact us at:

1-800-548-1029
or visit us at:
www.lifesjourney.org.

Father Tom's Parish Mission Talk

Believing and Living the Gospel
(Week 1)

The first series of talks that Father Tom and Don presents in giving a parish mission.

These talks allow us to change our guilts about the past and turn them into gratitude. Available on CD. Some of the subjects covered are:

1) Letting God Love Us
2) Making a Decision
3) Letting Go of our Fears
4) Becoming Responsible

How to Transcend Our Anger Into Forgiveness
(Week 2)

The second series that Father Tom presents in giving a parish mission.

Available on both CD and video. Some of the subjects covered are:

1) Practical Tools in Developing Family Spirituality

2) Owning and Letting Go of the Family Anger System

3) Connecting the Gospel and the Sacraments to Everyday Family Life

4) A Prayer Life that Enables One to Stay Centered on God's Love

The Journey from Fear to Faith
(Week 3)

The third series that Father Tom presents in giving a parish mission.

Available only on CD. Some of the subjects covered are:

1) Where Does Love Come From?

2) Where Does Fear Come From?

3) Finding God in Our Brokenness

4) The Working of God in Our Lives

Other Available CD's and DVD's

God Loves an Unmade Bed

This is an audio presentation of *God Loves An Unmade Bed* as read by Father Tom.

We come into the world connected to God, but become disconnected through fear as well as life's pain and struggles. In an uplifting manner, Father Tom takes an in-depth look at the capital sins and explores ways in which we can grow from these experiences. We all desire to be reconnected to God, and Father Tom talks about the journey and how we get reconnected. The spiritual journey requires that we understand what we need in our lives and Father Tom shares his "needs list" as an example which we can follow.

Understanding and Taking Charge of Our Personality (4 CD's)

Life teaches us that if we don't understand our history we will repeat it. This also applies to our own personal histories. When we don't comprehend why we are the way we are, we will repeat what was done to us by the preceding generation as well as pass it on to the next generation. We need to become familiar with the different defense mechanisms and personality traits that we have used to get by in life. This series presents our different habit systems: people pleaser, workaholic, perfectionist, victim or martyr, rescuer, and tap dancer. All these characteristics have positive and negative attributes that can greatly affect our behavior in relationships. How can we make these characteristics work for us rather than against us?

Family Spirituality (4 CD's)

As the marriage goes, so goes the family. As the family goes, so goes society.

Never before has the family unit been so threatened by outside pressures such as the vicious cycle of buying more yet never having enough. Today's family is so busy trying to provide economic security that there is little time or energy left for the family. In this series, Father Tom shows us how marriage is a living sacrament, a spiritual journey of two people growing in unconditional love for each other. When parents love each other unconditionally, they are giving the greatest gift to their children. In addition, when parents give the children what they need rather than what they want, the children develop a sense of belonging to a family. This important lesson not only strengthens the family but can boost a child's self-esteem. This series describes the stages of love between a couple, the pitfalls they may encounter, and tools to use in building healthy relationships. With a spiritual focus on the family, we can meet the challenges of today.

Step by Step (4 CD's)

Alcoholism is a spiritual disease that requires a spiritual recovery. It is important to note that although this series emphasizes alcoholism, its message can be applied to many other forms of compulsive behavior: the overeater, workaholic, sex addict, compulsive gambler, compulsive shopper, and so on. The series describes how 12-step programs work for these and many other compulsions and addictions. Such behavior patterns create the self-centeredness and self hatred that are at the core of spiritual disease. The 12-step program reveals the inner conversion of a person as he moves from self-centeredness to God-centeredness, and from self-hatred to self-esteem. This series details the first five steps of the 12-step program. This series can be an aid not only to the alcoholic or addict, but can serve an educational tool to other members of the family.

Spiritual Recovery from Drug and Alcohol Abuse
(4 CD's)

This series presents the materials mentioned above in STEP BY STEP, but from a different perspective. Instead of emphasizing the steps, these tapes present the disease as essentially rooted in co-dependency—our need to fill up the dark hole of our soul with people, places and things. The series presents a positive program of recovery by becoming our own best friend and finding God in this relationship. The great challenge of life is not learning to live with someone else, but learning to live with ourselves.

Life's Journey Mailing List

To be on our mailing list or email list and receive the latest information on Life's Journey books and CD's, or Father Tom's speaking engagements, please send your name and address to: Life's Journey, 12307 E. 53 St., Kansas City, MO 64133. Or email to: mail@lifesjourney.org. We can also be reached at 800-548-1029.

To schedule a mission at your church,
contact us at:

1-800-548-1029

or call Father Allendar at
1-415-310-5031

Or Call Sister Agatha
620-474-1135

Donald C. Fisher
&
Fr. Tom Allender
12307 E. 53 St.
Kansas City, MO 64133

www.lifesjourney.com

— NOTES —